The Book Cover

I named this book "BEHIND THESE WALLS" because I lived in these prisons and county jail. and the things I've seen that happen to the weak. Raped, robbed and stabbed. I had to have my "RELIGIOUS & SPIRITUAL FAITH" to protect me and keep me safe. I know for a fact

if I didn't have any faith in the Lord I would have been one of them guys on the ugly end of the stick. I'm happy that I was lead to see them guys getting baptized in Chino prison and that when my spiritual protection started for me in these prisons.

buffing weights "IRON" on the weight pile is a place where I bonded with my homies and where I let out to get the stress out with doing harm to other convicts.

Sitting in these cells over so many years I had time to think on what I'm going to do with my life or what kind of day I'm going to have once the door open. Being in prison has always kept me on my toes and alert to my prison surrounding because something could jump off at any time.

When one is going in and out prison the years fly by so fast and you wonder where did that time go?. As one knock down them calendar and get older in age this is time that we can never get back and get a start over.

I know that I had to stayed prayed up at all times BEHIND THESE WALLS.

BEHIND THESE WALLS

All Rights Reserved

No Part of this book may be reproduced or trans meitted, downloaded, reverse engineered, or stored in or introduced into information storage and retrieval system, in any form or by and means, including photocopying and recording, whether electronic or mechanical, now known or hereinafter invented without permission in writing from the author and publisher.

Front cover designed by Ojore Dhoruba Ajamu. Back cover designed by "Carlitos".

Photo credits by Ludis.

ISBN 9798748058810

Author Albert "Ru-Al" Jones

"BEHIND THESE WALLS"

BY

ALBERT "RU-AL" JONES

The contents of this work including, but not limited to, the accuracy of event, people and places depicted; opinions expressed; permission to use previously published materials included; and any advice given or cations advocated are solely the responsibility of the author, who assumes all liability for said work and indemnifies the publisher against any claims stemming from publication of the work.

DEDICATION

I dedicate this book to the Jones' family,
my daughter Albanisha, my grandson Eugene,
My grandson Emarih, my granddaughter
Emeire, and all my relative,
My homeboys and homegirls that walked
in these prisons.

Thank you for that true Love.

** GANGSTA BLOOD WORDS **

    Growing up in a gang neighborhood, or going into the county jails and prisons, these are places where one can get deeply immersed into these gangs and their lifestyles. It's a family unit that is much different from our real family on the streets.

    In these gangs we come up with our own language that only we can understand. Lawyers, doctors, police, prison guards, the military armed forces, college students -- all have their special way of communicating. Because mines and so many others are in a street gang don't make the others better than the others.

    Race plays a big part in how we communicate. Blacks talk in Swahili. Mexicans talk in Spanish. Whites use sign language. Prison guards talk in codes on their radios. No matter what team you're on you have that special line of communication that only you understand, and it keeps the car running smoothly.

    As you will see in this book words that start with "c", "s", and "k" we Bloods exchange those letters and replace them with a "b" -- it makes our language very unique, which we as B-dogs are.

    So I'm going to bick back and be bool while I drink a hot bup of boffee and smoke a bigarette in my bell, Blood.

            *   *   *

DICTIONARY OF GANGSTA WORDS

BLOOD WORD	MEANING
BLOOD	B-DOG, RADS
Y.G.B.	YOUNG GANGSTA BLOODS
CRIPS	CRABS, ERECKETS, FILTHY MACK NASTIES
COMPTON	BOMPTON
COUNTY JAIL	BOUNTY JAIL
SEE	BEE
COFFEE	BOFFEE
COOL	BOOL
KICK-IT	BICK-IT, "HANG OUT"
CIGARETTE	BIGARETTE, "SMOKES"
GIVE IT UP	GANG SIGNS WITH FINGERS
KOOL-AID	BOOL-AID
CUP	BUP
CRAZY	BRAZY
WET FORTY	$40 MONEY FOR VISITS
JUTE BALLS	DRY FOOD HIGH IN PROTEIN
SICK DICK	DISEASE
BED ROLL	BLANKET, SHEETS, SOAP, TOOTHBRUSH AND TOOTHPASTE
SIZE	MUSCLES, YOKES, BUFF
BUFFING	LIFTING WEIGHTS
SWOLE	MUSCLES, YOKES
QUARTERS	25 LBS. WEIGHT PLATES
SKINNY SCARY	AFRAID, EAT CHEESE
FIGHTING	"GET THEM UP"

BLOOD WORD	**MEANING**
ROBBED	JACKED
STOLE	HIT FIRST IN FACE
ROAM-ROAMING	BEING OUT OF CELL
CATWALK	LONG GLASS WALKWAY FOR OFFICERS ONLY SEE IN CELLS
BUSTERS	COWARD, SCARY, EATING CHEESE
P.C.	PROTECTIVE CUSTODY
DEEP	LOTS OF HOMIES
DIRT NAP	IN GRAVE, "DEAD"
CAR	GROUP OR GANG
S.A.	SPANISH-AMERICAN
C.O.	CORRECTIONS OFFICERS
NEIGHBORHOOD	HOODS
T-ROLLED	KNOCKED-OUT
HEAT	KNIFE, SHANK
RAT-PACKED	JUMPED ON
BLOOD MODULES	3600, 4300, 4600
TIERS	ABEL, BAKER, CHARLIE, DENVER
CUZZ	CRIPS' SAYING
WOLFING	TALKING TRASH
SAG -- SAGING	PANTS HANGING BELOW THE BUTT
GRAY GOOSE	PRISON TRANSPORT BUS
KITE	PRISON NOTE OR LETTER

*   *   *

CONTENTS

Introduction..i
Acknowledgment..ii

L.A. COUNTY JAIL...1
THE BLOOD MODULES...23
PRISON LIFE...90
THE COURT SYSTEM...187
HOMEBOYS & HOMEGIRLS.....................................189
DAMUISM..192
CALIFORNIA PRISONS.......................................193
PRISON ROLL CALL...194
S.O. DEATH ROW...197
S.O. DAMU ROLL CALL......................................201
MY PRISON PRAYER...202
EPILOGUE...203

INTRODUCTION

I'm RU-AL From Athens Park Bloods by way of Jarvis Street Mafia Pirus. I welcome you behind these walls with me. you will see the life that I lived and the way I made all the right moves so the I don't come out on the bad of most of the things that happen in here to other guys. I had to learn and get tough real fast and did just that. I couldn't get soft when I saw someone get beat down or saw them come out of their cell after being raped. I couldn't show no sad emotions for them because got what they had coming.

I never wanted to be a hard blood. I wanted to be a down one and smart one and I'm just that. So I say this, when you read this book, it's all real, every word, every fight, every beat-down and every heartbeat . it got ugly at times and it also got good in so many ways. you will know all there is to know about RU-AL BEHIND THESE WALLS.

ACKNOWLEDGMENT

This book is based on all true stories and every name is a real person who did this time with me. I'm giving them all their utmost most respect and i know it's about me and my legacy and the ones that made it possible along with their legacy I thank Y'all for that time you gave to groom me into a blood that know and understand how to do time. From my first time in 3600 blood module i listened to every word you said. Big Mouse A.P.B., Big Pudden 92 Bishop, China Dog L.L.P., Too-Kool L.A. Brim and Lumber Jack B.H.. When I walked into the modules and i wasn't from your hood Y'all still gave me the time to talk to me and because of that love I thank you O.G.s. I looked, listen and did less talking and here I am telling me story to you. Y'all taught me about loyalty, trust, understanding, respect love to all bloods and i took all that to with me, and some.

I give my utmost respect to all the homies that had my back. you was there when the smoke clear. and for that blood RU-AL is grateful because i enjoyed ridding beside you. i know that you put your life on the line for me as well as I did for you.

I know when this book hit your hands there will be some that will hate on the "RU" but I know that you will protect my name like i would yours.

I send my thanks to the whole Jones family. I love everyone to TAY who played the daddy role for me with my daughter for me. to my

ACKNOWLEDGMENT

baby girl Albanisha, you have been a big help to me and i thank you. When I got your first letter saying "DADDY" I love you and will always be with you, that touched my heart. I'm sorry that i missed so much of your life you're always my number one lady.

Daddy and Mamma I always felt your love and prayers for me as I lived my life in these prison but you knew that I would be safe in these prisons. To hear that Mamma voice on the phone really made me feel good thank you.

Judy you put up with so much with me running the streets and going in and out of prison. I knew that you had a lot of love for me and my gangsta life style and I thank you and our church "United Church Of The Living God" for having my back. I also thank my Mother-in-law, "MRS. JOHNSON" your love went a long way. But no matter what, your stupid face love you.

To our allies, you have played a big part in our bond in these prisons and i thank you for all that, and B-dogs thank you for that love and support. Let's not lose that bond because that side "CRIPS" don't have their's anymore and if they do, it is not as strong as ours.

To my sister Connie, you have been my backbone from the day I was born. I love you Ludis, Rinesha, Peanut 2, Nasha, Tiff, Relley, Tee, Suga, Bay-Bay, Lil Prentes, Shameka, Nadia, Shareen, Mitchshalae, Lil Paul, Johnnay, and all the rest of my family. I

ACKNOWLEDGMENT

Fell your love everyday I'm in here and I send mines.

To everyone who had a part in my life, keep your prayers coming my way. I need them, and God Bless you from behind these walls.

CHAPTER ONE

(L.A. COUNTY JAIL)

" get up men, your stay at Carson substation is over, you're being transfered to L.A. county jail in twenty minutes. So used the rest room now because there is no toilet on the bus." the jailer said. I have been in this for two days, i got caught up in the many raids that were going on throughout all of L.A. county because of the Olympic games. I was caught selling weed to an undercover cop. It's six other guys in this cell with me just one other black guy three Mexicans and two White dudes and they look like that are here for drinking because they slept all two days.

this is my first time being in jail this long and I know that Mamma is not going to bail me out. so now i got to through the court system to out but i heard that it's not good for drug dealers. I'm hoping that i get some short time this being my first time in the courts. I was the second guy to come into this cell and when these other guys came it stunk in her, like feet, musk, and ass. and I had to lay on the paper thin mattress and one blanket that made your skin itch. the food is nasty, no salt. it's plain with no taste at all. I did need the sleep. i had been running the streets and getting high. I did need a break from smoking "PREMOES" Rock Cocain mixed with weed. I hope when I get out I don't mess with them any more. The guards never turned the light off in this cell. that made it hard to sleep and the jailer would never tell us the time so we didn't know if it was day or night. We got all that from

BEHIND THESE WALLS

the new guy that came in he knew if it was day or night and the time.

I never been in a cramped place like this with six other guys. I had to listen to all that snoring and the flushing of the toilet that don't sound like a house toilet. this one sounded like the water was being splashed in the cell. no hot water and they had this stainless steel mirror on the wall that you can't see your face. I have not brushed my teeth in two days and I know that my breath is stinking and this nasty ass food maid it worse. they made me take off my shoes and put them on the other side of the glass door. When we wasn't sleeping or eating we would talk. and this one guy told me that they "COURTS" had three days to get me into court or it will be a D.A. "district attorney" reject and they will let me go.

So if i don't go to court in the morning I'll go home. "okay men it's time to go. when I call your name step up and give me your first name, and walk out to the hallway and put your left shoulder on the wall. Jones.' the jailer said with a very stern voice. "Albert" I said. i walked out the cell as i was told to do. they had about thirty other guys already in the hallway, cuffed up in this long ass line. I'm looking to see if I know anybody and I don't. I see that they did a big ass sweep on the streets. i know that all the other substations are full of people too. I get handcuffed to three other guys from my cell. I'm nicking for a cigarette I heard that we can smoke once we get to the county jail.

L.A. COUNTY JAIL

I can't wait to smoke one.

" Everybody walk forward to that door and step on the bus." the jailer said. when I got outside the sun was shinning. I heard someone say "it's 7:15pm." i looked at the side of the bus. it said "Los Angeles County Jail." the bus black and white like a police car. it had these bars wrapped around the whole bus that covered all the windows. i stepped on the bus and got a seat by the window. we had to do a lot of moving with four people on this chain. We pulled out of the parking lot and I could see the Carson mall. driving on the 1-10 freeway we went pass El Segundo and I can see the hood and I'm looking for someone i know but I didn't see anyone. Riding on the freeway I'm looking at all the houses and the people walking around. I'm wondering what they are doing since I lost my freedom. We go passed the Coliseum and the Olympic games are going on. looking at all these different hoods from this bus seat damn L.A. is big. I'm wishing i could be out there with them than on this bus. We get downtown. I'm trying to look at the skyscrapers. they seen so far away in the sky. people are walking around in suits doing their thing without any worries, at least it don't show. at least they are not going to a mad house like I'm about to encounter.

The bus pulled off the freeway. we get to this building and i see this sign that say. " Sherman block Sheriff Department." the bus pulled up into this big parking lot where i see fifty to sixty buses parked. when the bus stopped the two officers got off and

L.A. COUNTY JAIL

went to this window and gave them some paperwork.

Five officers came outside and one of them got on the bus and said " everyone stop talking, I'm only going to tell you once. when you get off the bus I want you to walk through that door over there where you see that officer standing. he will you what to do next. if you as you're told we could have you in bed by midnight. or you can make it last until 6:00am when I'll be going home.

I'm nervous as hell. we walk into this room with no walls but all glass windows. we was told to step on this yellow line that went all around the room floor. once everybody got on the line we're facing the window and the five officers started taking off the handcuffs. once the cuff were off we turned around and there was one officer standing in the middle of us. he was a short man and thin. he said. "okay men, first you address us as officers. we are not your home boys and friends. so when i ask you to do something i want it done and if we any problems we got a spot to deal with it so it's up to you on how you want to be treated. I want everyone to take off your shoes and clothes and put them in front of you. put all your personal property in one pile next to your clothes, your money, jewelry and glasses so make sure you got everything out of your pockets. now take one step in front of your property. If you have false teeth take them out of your mouth and hold them in your hand. everyone open your mouth and let these two officers look into to your mouth. okay now lift up your arms, now lift up your dicks and balls. now turn around and bend over and spread your butt cheeks and cough three times. okay lift up your feet so i can see the bottom of them. now get back behind your things. you five guys step forward and take out your braids and ponytails and then run your fingers through your hair. now step back." I had ponytails in my hair and other black guys had braids. i looked to the and I see these two big boards with about five hundred golf hat emblems. they took off guys golf hats when they came in here. Damn that's a lot of emblems.

I never seen anything like this before. some home boys told me of some of the things that happen in here. they left this part out. this is very degrading. i really fell less of a man, disrespected to the fullest. to bend down and spread my ass cheeks and cough and to hear all these dudes do the same this is some sick shit. standing here in front of all these other men. the only i did this was in junior high school locker room and even then I had my drawers on. and here I am lifting up my balls for another man to look at them. A different officer took over he had a softer voice. he had placed some green bags in front of us. Still standing there naked he said. " men you see that green bag that is placed in front of you, i want you to put all your clothes in it and put your other things in that small clear bag, That's money and your jewelry everything else leave on the floor because you can't keep it. when you get to that table over there with that officers he will have your money put on your books, you're allowed to have forty dollars

L.A. COUNTY JAIL

and then you can buy all the things that you need once you get to were you're going to be housed. once you're done with that, step to the side so you can be fitted for your county blues" (clothes).

i seen a lot of guys with money. i had none, they took mine when I got arrested for possession of sales. The officer called these three guys in brown clothes and said. "these guys are my trustees don't ask them for anything. they will ask you your clothes sizes and you tell them that and if you get the wrong sizes that's on you because they will not get any others. you will get your county blues, socks draws, t-shirt, and a bed roll and one fish kit with all your hygiene. once you get your clothes you will be able to take your shower. after you give my trustees your size, go sit on the bench until they come with your clothes." Sitting on this cold bench still naked I hoped they would hurry up with them clothes. after an hour they came with our clothes. I got mine and they fit just fine. I hear a few guys complaining that some thing don't fit. they had to wear it any way. everyone got dressed and then we was told to get in this long line and the officer said. " you will get your wristband and whenever an officer call your name you give him your last three numbers. once that is done you will be able to take your showers" cool, i hope this goes by fast because i need a shower real bad.

We walked to the area and there are two long wooded boxes with about forty squares where you can put your clothes. the officer Said. " when you get undressed step over here so I can spray you

L.A. COUNTY JAIL

for crabs and lice." He is standing next to this fifty gallon drum with some kind of pump on the top of it. It's a see through drum and i see some brown liquid in it.

looking at them guys go before me, and that shit is cold guys is running to the shower. i looked at the showers and it's only twenty shower heads for thirty five guys it's going to be a lot of bumping i know not t6o drop my soap. now it's my turn Damn, this shit is cold and it's got some kind of crazy smell to it. I was told to run my fingers through my hair. he then sprayed my private parts and off to the shower i went. it feel good to be talking a shower. I walked back to where my clothes we're. I'm drying off and I notice somebody put their money in their shoes I didn't even look around to see if anyone was looking at me, i stuck my hand in his box and grabbed the money and i walked to the other side of the locker. i put the money in my sock and i tied up my Chuck Taylors real tight.

I don't have a mirror to look at my hair but i know that my Jheri curl is all stringing and I hope that the sell curl activator. i got dressed and this white guy. said " who stole my money?." no body said any thing my heart is beating fast hoping no-one Say " he got it" no-one spoke and then the officer said " I told you to protect your things. now everyone get dressed so we can move on. we got a long ways to go." the guy is looking at everyone. he done know how got his money. I know that i got this big ass knot in my shoe, i didn't count it but it had to be forty dollars. he got

BEHIND THESE WALLS

caught slipping not protecting his money.

We moved to this other room where there are about fifteen steel benches. the officer said. " men i want y'all to straddle the bench. I want y'all to be nuts to butt so every body can sit. it's 12:45am and I'm going to feed you. after you're done eating you will be seen by the doctors. there you will tell them about any illness you may have or if you're on any type of medications. if you don't and you get sick that's on you. mu trustees will bring you your food and some coffee and once again do not talk to them. and the sooner you see the doctors the faster you can get to the nine thousand floor and get you bed." I hope so because i'm sleepy. I notice that them black dudes never talked to me they just hung out with each other. they must be some crabs. i looked over at them and one gave me a nod and then gave up a big ass "C" with his fingers. i shook my head no and gave up a "B". one crab gave me a smerk so i gave him one back. they all are my size and age but i know i can fuck up two of them. i know that they are going to rat pack my ass. if so all i want to do is get one or two of them first. i know if anyone of them get in my face i'm going to steel (punch) on him first.

Six trustees had set up two long tables and they had food and coffee on them. I walked up and got mine and sat back down. i opened up the plastic bag and it's a big ass ham sandwich with a thick piece of cheese. I'm so hungry i fucked that sandwich up and

BEHIND THESE WALLS

dranked that nasty ass coffee. after everyone was done the trustee came in and picked up all the trash. I'm sitting there not talking to no-one so i un-rolled my bed roll and took out my fish kit to see what was in it. a small tooth brush, tooth paste, a thin ass comb no way i'm going to be able to comb my hair, this comb is for white boys and Mexicans. As my hair is drying it's starting to nap up. a bar of soap that would only last through on shower. one sheet, one blanket and this cloth sack to cover the mattress. I rolled it back up. it's been thirty minutes since we ate and the door has been closed all that time. I was expecting them crabs to say something to me but they didn't.

the door opened and this oriental officer walked in and he said. " this is the last stage of this process before you get to your bunks. you're going to walk through that door over there, you will get your photos taken, chest ex-rays, weighed and then your blood taken. after all that you will see the doctor if you have any S.T.D.s or those that don't know what that mean if you have sick dick, tell the him and you will be taken care of. once you're done you will walk back through that door and sit back down and then you're off to the nine thousand floor."

I walked up to get my photo taken. he took three of them. i got my chest ex-rayed that thing was cold on my chee-chee bird chest. I got on the scale and i weighed one hundred and twenty two pounds.

BEHIND THESE WALLS

I'm standing in line to get my blood taken away from me. I don't see any doctor, they are making you stick your arm through this hole in the window that is covered up and there's no way to see what's going on, they could be putting a disease in my body. I don't like needled but I got to do it. I stuck my arm in and i felt the needle go in. I held my breath and when he or she was done I let that breath out. I walked to the doctor sitting at the table ha said. "MR. Jones do you have sick dick?." I said "no". he told me to go back in to the room. I'm glad that is over with.

Both door are closed. i seen what time it was it's 3:40 in the morning. i'm so sleepy i want to lay down so bad. It's been a long day and night, now it's morning. the door opened up and two officers waled in. the short said. ' Okay when I call your mane give your last three and stand on the yellow line outside this door. there will be an officer. he will tell you what to do. I will be making three lines so listen up because i"m only going to call your name one time".

As the name are being call the other officer is handing people this green card and telling then which line to stand in. out of nowhere the officer yelled at this white dude. he said. " asshole didn't i tell you to get your dumb ass in line two? why do you have your body in line three?." He walked up to the dude and pushed his face to the wall. and then four other officers came and they took him to this room and I could hear the guy screaming. they is beating his

L.A. COUNTY JAIL

ass. the officer said. " see what happen if you don't listen? this is my house you're not doing the shit that you was doing on the streets so let's start again." my name is called. i got up, gave him my last three numbers and was told to get in line three. I made sure i didn't get fucked up because that dude got his ass beat. I'm in line with six other guys. all of the crabs was in line one.

Once the last person was called and place in line. the six officers that that just beat dude up came back. one spoke up real loud. " men in line one follow these two officers, your going to be housed in ninety five hundred." one officer got in the front of that line and the other one followed behind him. the second group of guys went to ninety three hundred and they left tow minutes after the first group.

I'm standing in the Hallway with four other guys. I wonder why we was put in this group and not the others. the last two officers was standing in the hallway talking to each other. then one said. " you guys have a date wit the judge this morning. you will get housed when you get back. so when you pass that big blue bend up there put your bed roll in there. you will get a new one once you get back. don't worry, the officer will know you don't have a bedroll okay. now lets go."

Me and the other guys was put into a cell not knowing what was next. I'm thinking about the pass four hours how i went through that human assembly line as if I was some kind package in a ware house being tossed around. That shit was crazy and to see that dude

L.A. COUNTY JAIL

get his ass beat for being in the wrong line. I don't think that I could do this again. i got to find something else to do on them streets and my life or I'll be right back in here. i felt so disrespected in every way and there wasn't anything i could do unless i want what that dude got. I was told how these officers in here act, they will kick you ass. they try to get their reputations before they get to the streets. so I'll pass on the ass kicking part and stick to their program because i know that i can't win.

"Excuse me officer do you have the time?." I asked. the officer sitting at the desk said. " it's 4:50am. an officer is on his way to take Y'all to the chow hall to eat breakfast and then you will be placed in your court tank so be patient men." "thank you" I said.

Twenty minutes an officer walks up and says " lets go to the chow hall. get in on line and walk this way. I'll be on the side of you."

We get to the chow hall and it's packed with people that is going to court. I get in line and the officer said. "when you're done eating walk back where you just came from and stop at the desk and give that officer you name and number and he will tell you what court you will be going to and what court tank to go to."

The line is going fast. i see all these trustees doing all the work and no officers around them and a lot of guys in line is talking to them. I hear one dude ask a trustee for some cigarettes and the

L.A. COUNTY JAIL

black guy working gave him a nod. i got to where that trustee is said. " can I get a smoke?." he said " yeah i got packs for five dollars and singles for twenty five cents, so what do you want?." I want a pack and some matches" I answer. He said " okay when you come with your empty tray someone will be there to give you the smokes, make sure you have the money ready." he said all this in a low tone of voice as he put the food on my tray. I gave him the okay nod and moved on. I looked at the food and it looked ten times better than the substation food. it was gravy with some ground beef in it and diced potatoes and two biscuits, oatmeal, an apple and a small carton of milk. I ate everything but not the oatmeal. I never did eat oatmeal or grits.

I notice there was two officers on each end of the table telling people to get up. if you wasn't done you had to eat the rest while you're walking to the trash can. I took a five dollar bill out of the forty dollars in my shoe. I put the rest back in my shoe so I don't get robbed. I'm looking at the guy that was talking to the trustee so i can do the right thing.

I get to the trash can and this black dude looked at me and winked. I got the money balled up in my hand, he gave me the pack of camels and I handed him the money and I dumped my tray and put my hands in my pockets. I remember what that officer said " whenever you walk these halls always have your hands in your pockets, because if you don't others will think that your going to do something to them."

I'm walking, following these other guys and they got their shoulder

L.A. COUNTY JAIL

Close to the wall so i did the same thing. i got to the desk and gave the officer my name and number, he said " Jones you're going to Compton court. go to tank sixteen and wait for the officers to come get you." I found tank sixteen and about twenty five guys are already in there and it is smoked out. I don't go right in. I take a walk around to look at where I'm at and it about fifty of these tanks and there is people in everyone of them. it's loud and smokey I walked back to my tank. I go in and found a nice spot to sit so I can see the front gate. I lit a smoke and that first hit got me dizzy. on the streets I smoked Kools menthols.

the tank is full and it's standing room only. guys is talking to each other. It's now so packed with people no more can come in, they was sent to another tank. I don't see any bloods but there are a few crips in here. I'm sure that they know that I'm a blood because I won't talk to them. I might not look like a blood my hair is so jacked up. That spray stuff got my hair so dry that i don't have one curl in my hair. I know that I'm looking like a smoker or a bum, that's cool. that just might keep these crabs from rat packing me.

sitting in this hot ass tank for an hour now and i got to take a piss but if I get up I'll lose my seat. I'll hold it until it's time to go. an officer came to the tank and no-one could hear him, then he said. " everybody shut the fuck up, when i call your name step up and give me your last three and walk to that officer to get

BEHIND THESE WALLS

Handcuffed." people was getting handcuffed real fast. I used the rest room. I'm following everybody else so i don't fucked up. standing in a four man chain the officer counted everyone in line. one minute later we're walking pass all these tanks that's full of people. we get outside and the fresh smelled so good. it's a real crisp morning. We're walking toward one of many buses. by me being last in line I was seated in the front of the bus. The driver said. " I don't want no smoking on my bus, if I smell it I will take all you cigarettes and you will not get them back. you can talk but not too loud because I will have the radio on, if it to loud i will cut it off.

The cage door got closed, it separated us from the two officers. I'm looking out the window as we're leaving the county jail bus parking lot. I see these guys in powder blue jump suits. I asked this guy next to me who they was. he said. " those guys only have about six month to nine months to do. they are special trustees. they work outside the jail."

We get on the freeway and just like a blink of an eye we pull under the court building into this garage. once in it the door closed the bus got turned off and the two officers got out and put their guns in this locker that is on the wall. they both walked inside. While on the way here them crips back there seem like every word that came out their mouth was cuzz. I didn't trip they wasn't talking to me.

BEHIND THESE WALLS

The bus door opened and these court officers stepped on and said, okay men, when you step off the bus go in and face the wall so you can be un-cuffed and put into your tank." the cage door opened and the officer stepped to the side by the driver's seat as he watched everyone get off the bus. I'm facing the wall to get my cuffs off. it's about ten to fifteen court officers to take off the cuffs. this big black officer said. " when you have one cuff off put that hand on the wall and then the other one and leave them up there until i tell you otherwise. okay take them down and turn around. for you that have your store stuff (FOOD) with you, place it on this desk and I'll make your name on it and you will get it on your way back to the county jail. If your a crip step forward. put them in tank three. if your a blood step forward, put them in eight." I was the only one that stepped up. I looked at them crips and one of them smiled at me and gave me a nod. the officer told me to follow him. I did. we walked around the corner and he then opened the door. i walked in. it's seven other bloods sitting in there and two was laying on the floor. this tank was very small. I greeted everyone with the b-dog hand shake.

I sat on the floor and lit a smoke. we started talking about the streets and two of them been on the J-block before. I didn't know any of them, the homie from Fruit Town Piru is fighting a murder case of a crab. He asked me what I was in for. I said. " selling weed, i got caught up in those raids that is going on out there." he said. " RU-AL you should get about twenty days since this is

BEHIND THESE WALLS

your first time in the courts." Two other homies are in trial for killing crips. My shit is very small compared to their's. These bloods is fighting for their lives but they seem cool and calm. They put in some real work on them crabs. I told the homies that i have been up for 24 hours and that I needed some sleep. Jinks said. " RU-AL you will be going to 3600 blood module. did you ever go to O.S.S.?." I said "no, what's O.S.S.?." " that stand for Operation Safe Streets. They are gang detectives that work only with gang members, and you got to see them before you can go into the blood module, so when you go back ru-al you won't be going to the nine thousand floor. also you want to come to the module. your big home boy is in there, Big Mouse. you don't want to go to the nine thousand floor by your self it's full of crabs and if they catch any b-dogs up there they will get you. so your lucky that you came to court first." Jinks said.

I' glad that Jinks and the other home boys put me up on what to do. and the program. now i know what to do when I get back. I'm learning all I can, this being my first time in the county jail. I know this it's hundred time different from the streets. I know once i get to the module I'm going to meet a lot of new b-dogs.

" MR. Jones step out, it's your time to see the judge." the officer said. I got up and my heart is beating fast. buy why?. they are fighting murder cases and they are cool and calm. i can';t help it this is my first case. on the way out the door Jinks Said. " B-up ru-al." "okay blood." I said. I follow the officer. we get to the elevator and when we walked in it was packed with people. I see two of them crabs and three girls that was going to court. when we got off the elevator everyone was put into this big holding tank with a phone and the girls went down the hall. i was put in a small tank by myself. and no phone. I lit a cigarette. I hope i get the twenty days like the homis Jinks said i could get.

I hear a key go into the door and it's for me. the officer walked me into the courtroom. it's so big in here the judge is behind this big ass desk an old white man and he looks mean. standing there this short white man walked up to me and stuck out his hand and said. " hi I'm your public defender MR. Thomas, we are going to see if i can get you some county time, by this being your first offence." I said. " okay" the clerk called my name and case number and my lawyer spoke up and said. MR. Jones is present with counsel your honor. This is MR. Jones first time in the court system and his first felony, i talked to the district attorney and he agreed that MR. Jones do twenty days in the county jail." The judge said. " does the D.A. agree with these terms?." " yes your honor i do agree with these terms." the D.A. said. "okay, Mr. Jones i sentence you to twenty days in the county jail and i give you credit for three days, that leaves you with seventeen days left. Good luck Mr. Jones i hope i don't see you in my courtroom again. you're not going to be so lucky. I hope you get your life together, do you understand Mr. Jones?." the judge said. I answer. "yes your honor."

L.A. COUNTY JAIL

I get back to the holding tank and three of the homie are gone to the courtrooms for their trials. Jinks is still in the tank. he said. " how much time did you get ru-al?." I didn't want to say knowing that I'm going home in seventeen days and he could get life in prison so I said. " twenty days." he said. " I told you blood that you would get a little time. you will be on the first bus back to the bounty jail after lunch. and they are going to take you right to the blood module and from there you will go to O.S.S. before you get a cell." Jinks said.

One thing i notice about these bloods when they talk, words that start with a "C" they replace with a "B" and some words that start with a "S" they do the same. now i remember in high school some homies talked like that but these bloods has a good flow with their talk.

Me and the homie Tray caught the early bus back. we was put in the front of the bus in these two men cage. he told me this is how they try to keep us away from the crabs. He said. " once we get to the bounty jail all bets are off so be ready blood." I said. " oh I'm down to ride on some crabs. that's my thang." tray only has six months to do. he was happy to get that time. he got a nice jheri curl and he's about my size and the same age. he told me that he's on able row. he said. " if you get on that row i could let you use some of my curl activator and I'll braid your hair up for you. I see that that spray got your hair all fucked up. and you will get a care package." I said. "bool".

L.A. COUNTY JAIL

We get to 3600 blood module and I picked up and a new bed roll while i was downstairs. this officer that is sitting behind the desk said. " Tray go to your cell and don't be roaming. Mr. Jones you got to go to O.S.S. before you can get a bed so set your roll down by the wall and you walk down this hall, make a left and walk down this long hallway follow the red line to thew escalator. you ride it to the nine thousand floor and you will see a sign that points to O.S.S.. here take this green card and give it to the officer that's there. and you can call me officer McBEY." I said. "okay.". I think I understand what he just told me. I look down the tier and it was trash everywhere and real noisy like some kind of mad house.

Walking down this long hallway there are all kinds of paintings on the wall. I see these two officers yelling at this Mexican guy. the tall one is up in his ear yelling. I don't think that the Mexican guy understand english. right as i was passing them one officer slammed his face on the wall when his face left the wall there was blood coming down the wall. the officer did it again he had to have broken his nose because he got blood poring out like a faucet running water. the other officer had to be every bit of five foot four and he took his long ass flash light and hit the guy in the side. I never seen a flash light that long it had to have about eight to ten battery's in it. the Mexican guy is bent over in pain. he hit him so hard he couldn't scream. they grabbed him by his collar and shoved him on the wall again. the tall officer looked at

BEHIND THESE WALLS

me and said " what the fuck you looking at? do you want to be next? if not keep looking forward and walking." I turned my head away and picked up my pace. I don't want these crazy ass pigs to go crazy on my black ass.

I get to the nine thousand floor. i walked by ninety five hundred i was able to look inside and it's about two hundred dudes in there and bunk beds everywhere. I see the blacks got one side and the Mexicans are on the other side. I know it's a lot of crips in there. i know i would have got rat packed for sure if i went in there.

I walked up to this door that got a sign on it that said O.S.S. with a sheriff star. i knock on the door and this white officer with a green jacket on that said. " L.A. Sheriff" on the back. he said, ; come on in ru-al jones we are waiting for you. did you get lost?.' I said. "nope." I'm not about to tell them what I just seen. he said. " okay Mr. Jones i see that your a blood from A thens Park Bloods and your allies are the J-Block, Denver Lanes, Miller Gangsta Bloods, The Jungles and all the Pirus hoods, your gang name is "RU-AL". You just got twenty days, so you won't be here too long. I will house you in 3600 Blood module. I know your wondering how i know all this about you. Well i worked the gang details for ten years on the streets, so i know just about every gang member out there. now i control all gang activities in this jail. How is your home boy Cyclone?. we go way back" I said. " he's bool." I'm surprise that he know bloods like that. I looked on the wall and the whole side is covered with blood's photos, hundreds of them, and on the other side are hundreds of crips photos and there are some Mexicans and a few of some white dudes and everybody is giving up their hoods (GANG SIGNS). "okay ru-al let's take your flick and give up your hood." he said. I didn't smile, I gave my mean look and gave up Athens park and after that he said. " RU-AL you can go back to 3600 blood module to your home boys and I hope that they school you (TEACH) proper because you never been in anything like this before and I don't want any shit out of you while you're in my house."

Going by ninety five hundred some dues came to the window there is no glass. on said " What's up cuzz where your from?." I looked at them smiled and gave up a big ass "P" sign. them dude went nuts. oh i know for sure that they would have beat my ass to death in there. walking back down the long hallway i se the blood is still on the wall and there is a trail of blood on the ground where they must have took that Mexican dude. I know they fucked that man up.

I walked pass this trustee and he is shining this officer's boots and there is two other officers waiting to get their boots shine. Damn they have trustee for everything in here. I get to the door of 3600 I took two deep breaths and walked in, this is where i will be living for the next seventeen days.

CHAPTER TWO

(THE BLOOD MODULES)

Officer Mcbey said. " ru-al you're on Able row cell ten, your big home boy Mouse is one of my trustees and he is on Baker row. I'm sure you will find a way over there to see him. grab your bed roll and walk down the tier and stand in front of your cell and I'll let you in." My heart is still beating fast this all new to me. I got my bed roll under my left arm and I started down this dark tier. I walked passed the first cell and somebody said. " What's up blood, where are you from?." I said in a half-deep tone, " I'm ru-al from Athens Park." still walking every cell i passed someone is saying what's up. my heart is not beating as fast, i'm being greeted with a lot of blood love.

Standing in front of the cell i looked in and I see Tray. i was happy to see him. officer Mcbey got on the mic and said. " watch the gate, the gate is opening." i stepped inside and it is as dark as it is on the tier, i looked at the light and they have some news paper covering the light. once again officer Mcbey Said. " watch the gate, the gates are closing." the gate slammed shut and Tray got off his top bunk and gave me a hug and said. " this is Pudden from 92 Bishop, Too-Chille from fruit Town Brims, Rubber Legs from Denver Lane Gang." They all shook my hand and welcomed me to the cell. I put my stuff on the top bunk. I sat on Pudden's bunk and lit a smoke. it's a six man cell and thirteen cells on this row.

THE BLOOD MODULES

They started telling me about the everyday program. which is not much, but not bad. I smoked my cigarette and started making up my bed. once I was done I was given a care package. five candy bars, shower shoes, long tooth brush, tooth paste, big afro comb, two bars of dial soaps and a pack of Camels cigarettes and matches. Rubber Legs said, " ru-al this is how we treat our blood brothers, and if you need anything else just let someone know and we will try and get it for you." I smile and said. " thank you bloods".

Tray gave me some curl actavator for my dry ass hair. I must have used a whole tube to get my curls back and they all didn't come back. Tray did say that he would braid my hair in the morning. I told the homies that i need some sleep. I went to sleep and woke up at dinner time. All the cells got opened at the same time and every body came out to see the new blood (ME). I greeted with a hand shake and I made a "B" and "P" with my fingers and they all gave it back to me the same way. I learned even more gang signs with my fingers. I didn't expect this kind of love, but it was true blood love. " Watch the gates, the gates are closing." officer Mcbey said. We all got in line and walked out of the gang module to the chow hall. There are six officers walking with us. Just as the first time walking in a line I'm following someone else so I don't fuck up. once in the chow hall I grabbed a tray, I notice that we are the only ones in here. I got my food and sat down. It's mashed potatoes and gravy and a big piece of ham, green beans and two

BEHIND THESE WALLS

Slices of bread. I got a glass of red bool-aide which tasted crazy. I'm eating fast. I learned that from breakfast. I wanted some more Bool-aide. it was gone from the pitcher, one of the homies grabbed the empty pitcher and held it up and said. " juice man". this trustee came with a fresh pitcher of juice. Pudden said. " ru-al you like that Jim Jones juice?." "what's Jim Jones?." I asked. he laughed at me and said. " that juice you're drinking has soft peter in it, they put this powder mix in the juice so your dick won't get hard. they do that so guys don't have sex with other guys but that shit don't work because there are a lot of booty bandits in here. and the Jim Jones part is that dude that had all them people to drink that red juice and they all died in Africa. that's how the juice got it's name. so do you want some more?." I said. " hell naw blood I'm bool on that JIM JONES JUICE."

Pudden stood about six foot three and he have some size on him. he is a big blood. the only blood that I knew was that big is RU-Roger on Cook street and he is on monster swole. Pudden is a soft spoken blood and he took a liken to me. we get back from dinner and we're given and hour of tier time. that gave me time to see and talk to all the other bloods. just about all of them have murder cases. these b-dogs was putting in work on them crips. Some had dope cases and here I am with just seventeen days. not too many of these homies are going to get any short time.

back in the cell Pudden took the newspaper off the light and we're playing cards (SPADES) and drinking Boffee which we are using the milk carton for the cup. I see someone walk by with a broom, it was on of the homies, he's a tier trustee. he get to roam and pass things for us from cells to cells. Tray said. " we are going to get some day room time in about an hour. there we get to shower, used the phone and watch T.V.. We get that one hour and you better take your shower first because a lot of the homies like to used the phone first."

All the cells open for day room time. I went right to the shower and I see about ten shower heads and it's twenty guys in there all at one time. i seen this in the movies. this guy dropped his soap and when he bent over to pick it up he got gang raped. so I will be holding my soap tight. So that's where soap on the rope come from. I do remember what Pudden told me about the booty bandits in here. fresh out of the shower, now I need to used the photo and call home to let Mamma know what's up with me. I see Pudden on the phone. I asked him to let me use it after him he said. " okay".

" Hi mamma how are you doing?. I said. she said, " how are you doing in there son?. Lisa been over here everyday since you went to jail. So when do you come home?." I said, " I'm okay Mamma, I come home in seventeen days. mamma could you give Lisa my booking number so she can come see me. Mamma I got to get off the phone somebody else want to use it." "okay you be careful in there Albert, i keep on tell you son that them people is not playing with you. they will put you away forever if you don't start acting right see you soon". Mamma said. I hung up the phone and went and sat at a table by myself.

I'm looking at all these bloods they are enjoying themselves. this is a lifetime bond that's going on here, a bond of brothers with the same enemy's. I walked to some homies and they are telling war stories on how they shot up crips and got shot at by some crips. I'm telling mines and how i beat them up with my fist. This tall slim blood walked up and said. " what's up ru-al? I'm 187 from the jungles." he got some long ass braids that went to the middle of his back. I heard that he has a murder case too. I greeted him with the hand shake and we both gave up the "B". I looked to the other side of the day room and I see three guys laughing at something one of them said. I walked over to them and they stopped talking. I said. " What's up bloods I forgot Y'all names." One homie short and stocky, said. " I'm Jimbo that's Resse and the other homie is No Brains and we're all from (N.H.B.) neighborhood bloods 20s. We're just chillen, you might have heard us talking. we are all in cell twelve." I said. So what is y'all in for?." Resse said. " we were fighting some crabs murders and we got action to beat them." I walked away I'm like damn who don't have a murder case in here. I went back to the table I was just at and I'm looking at all these bloods and they are acting like they don't have a worry in the world and they might not ever get out again and they all are young.

Behind these walls

Day room time was bool, I'm back in my cell and I hear some Mexicans talking in Spanish. I asked Tray. " why are them Mexicans in here?. " Oh, they are Charlie row, they show us respect and we give it back to them. Your big home boy is on Bakers row I'll show you how to get over there in the morning." Tray said. " When do we get visits?. I asked. Too-Chille said. " we get visits on Mondays, Wednesdays and Saturdays. They are for only thirty minutes, if you go by your self you better watch out for them crabs on the main line. they be out there roaming looking for b-dogs to rat pack. They caught and few homies out there slipping so any ways be ready ru-al. I said. "okay blood."

I got my first good night sleep and i feel much better. Rubber Leg spoke. "blood i got to go to school today but I'm not going. Me and 187 is going up to the nine thousand floor to make some money." I said. " they got school, and y'all is going up there. What about the crabs?. " As for school i'm working on my G.E.D. and the teachers show us movies too. But today we're ditching school and about five of us is going up there, so we got enough homies to fuck up the crabs if they want some funk. We are going to rob the white boys." Rubber Leg. Said.

They came back after lunch and they got hundreds of dollars and 187 got on a brand new pair of tennis shoes. now they are in cell seven shooting dice and smoking weed. I'm looking at them and 187 passed me the joint and I hit it two times and started coughing. This is

Some good weed. I walked back to my cell with Tray and he said. " ru-al come with me I'm going to show you how to see you be home boy. you hang out right here, this gate will get open. and you just walk out the gate and go around that corner and your big homie is in cell four. Don't trip on the officer at the desk he's bool he'll let you in on Baker row. Somebody is coming get ready ru-al."

I'm nervous as hell. I walked through the gate and the officer at the desk let me on Baker row. all the guys are out on the tier having tier time. I met some more b-dogs. I get to cell four, standing in the front doorway. I looked in and i see this big ass black blood sitting on the bunk. His cell had to be as dark as our cell. he looked like he was in deep thought. I said. " what's up big mouse. i'm ru-al your homie off Carlton street." I stuck my hand out to greet him. He stood up, I'm like damn this is a big ass blood. I'm glad he's my home boy. He gave me a hug to my surprise. he said, " I know who you are. I heard that you was around here. how are they treating you?." "They are showing me a lot of blood love." i said. He spoke in a low voice. " That's good we got some good b-dogs in here. sit blood. do you know Ronald Gram?, he is on the other side in thirty five hundred on Denver Row. he's been there for two weeks now." "Yeah i do know him from Cook street but I didn't know that he was in jail." I said. Sitting on the foot of his bed. Big Mouse started talking about how to conduct myself as a blood in these jails and prisons. he's talking and I'm all ears. being in here is a hundred times different than the streets. to be so big he got a soft spoken voice, but it was stern. he got my full attention and his every words. he said. " ru-al, respect all bloods no matter what hood they are from and you will get the same respect. ru-al, behind these walls, the way to stay out of trouble is to look, listen and less talking. you will see a lot of guys that talk too much and end up saying the wrong things and that's when you have made your mouth your worst enemy. so the less you talk the better off you'll be." he stopped talking for a moment and he went into his pants and pulled out this red pouch. it got this long red string on it. he took out this fat as joint and handed it to me to light. I did. i took one big hit and i started choking. "Damn blood this shit is good." I said. He laughed at me. he seemed happy to have one of his little homies with him to talk to. He got back to schooling me after we smoked that fat ass joint.

"RU-AL you're going to come across some homies trying to recruit you." he said. I didn't understand what he was saying so he broke it down for me to understand. "What I mean by recruiting you. That's getting under paper work. there are U.B.N. UNITED BLOOD NATIONS, and there is B.L. BLOOD LINE. I know that you never heard of any of these names before but I must tell you about them. These are all bloods but your under their paperwork and structure. If you sign any kind of paperwork your in, this is called being under paperwork. and being under that you might be told to do something to another b-dog that you like and if you don't do it you will get dealt with for not following that order and it can get real ugly

THE BLOOD MODULES

For you. So i say again LOOK, LISTEN and LESS TALKING and you will be okay. I'm not tell you to join or not join that's up to you and how you want to do your time. but when you do decide, make sure you're one hundred present sure that's what you want. I love all blood and I'm down with them all. I chose not to join or get under any paperwork , I don't like or want to be separated from my blood brothers. you will see this in prisons so ru-al what do you think of what I just talked about?.he said. I said. " I never heard of any paperwork but I know this I don't want to be separated from my blood homies ever and from what you're saying i will, if I join. So I'm bool on that paperwork. stuff. I don't want to hurt another b-dog. wow that's some heavy shit right there. I'm okay. I'll just stay down with all bloods".

" Don't get me wrong ru-al there are good b-dogs on both sides you got to do your own thinking and decision making on that. I'm just letting you know so when you come to something like that you will understand and know what to do." Big Mouse said.

It's dinner time and I'm stuck on this side. I hope i don't get into any trouble. Big Mouse said. " you can come eat dinner with me. officer Mcbey is bool, he's not going to trip on you." After we ate we went back to his cell. I met his cellies . he went back to his pants and pulled out three red bags and he said. " ru-al here take this, this is a money bag. you keep your money in it and you can take a shower with it. so tie it on your draws and you sleep with your money and take it everywhere wit you. You don't have to

THE BLOOD MODULES

Keep your money in your socks any more. here is two joints for you to smoke on. also take this care package with you. I know that the homies looked out for you already but some of them are scandalous so don't just take everything someone give to you okay?. you got to remember that these guys are not in here for selling girl scout cookies, most of them are real killers and they feel they can get over on you they will so it's not bool to take everything you bee.

" It's time for count watch. all the gates are opening you got ten minutes to get to your cell for count so say your good byes." Mcbey said. big Mouse walked me to the gate and asked Mcbey to let me back on my tier and he did. Big Mouse gave me a big hug and said. " you're going to be okay little homie." and then he pointed to his temple and know what he is saying, THINK.

I get back to the cell. they got the spade blanket set up and ready to play cards. We drank boffee, smoked a joint and started talking shit. it's about eleven o'clock and we are still playing cards and out of nowhere I hear a loud scream. It stopped. two minutes later it started again but this time it's much louder. I said "blood who is that?." Too-Chilly said. " some body is getting fucked in the ass, this isn't the first night that this been going on. it's some dude in thirty five hundred on Denver row. when the screaming stopped that mean he got a dick in his mouth to keep him quiet." Tray stared laughing and said. " blood you'll have to kill me before i let someone fuck me in my ass that's on blood."

THE BLOOD MODULES

We stopped playing cards and I'm laying on my bunk and then that screaming started again I'm thinking why this dude is not fighting them?. they must have punked him so bad that he don't have no fight left in him, and he's scared to death and letting them rape him. It's late. I know that the officers hears that shit and why is he not going to check on that dude?. Well so much for the soft peter because it's not tonight.

four thirty in the morning and three homies is about to go to the Youth Authority (Y.A.). for the last two days all the been talking about is fucking up some crabs when they get down to the court tank. I heard one homie say. " blood it's going to a four fifteen in the morning (RIOT). We are going to shut the Bounty jail down." I can hear the three homies going to every cells saying their good buy's. I asked. Rubber legs how they going to know that they had a fight?." He said. " you see that clear plastic box on the wall right there?. when the bounty jail is on lock down, it's a red light that goes off and then they will stop all the movement in the jail and will know that the young homies got off on some crips. that's how you get your stripes and reputation behind these walls."

They lifted the lockdown and we got some tier time. I stayed in the cell laying on my bunk looking at the ceiling, getting some thoughts together, most of my thinking was on what big mouse had said to me. the things he told me really opened my eyes to a lot

BEHIND THESE WALLS

Because I could end up in prison and I don't want to be caught up in something that could get ru-al into a lot bad shit. out of nowhere i hear. " fuck you blood you're cheating. I'm no buster you can't just cheat me like that and get away." the voice said. Pudden said. "that's Yap from neighborhood twenty and 187 down there shooting dice. they fuss all the time, gambling can lead to someone getting seriously hurt, yeah it's okay to gamble, but you got to know when to stop. it can get other home boys into bad things. I've seen guys get stabbed for twenty five cents and it's not the amount but the principle. I say this homies and i'm talking to all y'all in this cell, there are things that can get into a lot of shit and maybe death. gambling, your mouth and bad dope deals is your worst enemy and fucking with them homosexuals them three things can get you killed behind these walls."

now i got some more information on how to act and what to look for while doing time. Big mouse and pudden both gave me some good words and they gave it to me and other young homies andit all came in threes so it's easy to remember. Big Mouse, look, listen, less talking. Pudden Gambling, talking and homosexuals, I'm taking their words and schooling to heart because this might not be the only time I come to jail.

It's late night and I can hear that screaming again. Why is that dude staying in that cell?. I'm sure he went to the chow hall where he could get away but here he is again screaming. he must like it

THE BLOOD MODULES

And the officers never stopped it or went to check or see who was screaming late night. That is some brazy shit. this place is not for the weak because if you're weak you will be screaming every night.

I wake up to get ready for my day. we ate breakfast. and know we are smoking my last joint. we passed it around. two hits and pass. we're high and i reach under the bunk to get my bag of food . I feel like eating some yum-yums. when I picked the bag up all the food fell out. all my candy have a bite mark on them. i said." blood who did this to my shit?. everybody started laughing, i didn't bee a damn thing funny. I'm mad Too-Chilly said. " blood you got robbed by freeway Freddy." " who and the hell is Freeway Freddy?. I asked. with all of them still laughing. Tray Said. " rual it's this rat that steal steals people food or do what he did to yours. he'll bite all you food and leave you mad as hell. he has never been caught no matter how many traps we set up. this rat find a way to outsmart us. you bee why we got our food hanging up on the bars? to keep Freeway Freddy's ass away. So next time, put your stuff on the shelf or tie it up and hang it on the bars."

Officer got on the mic and he announce all the visits and my name was called for one o'clock and i know it's Lisa and her moms. The homie Tray hooked my hair up with some braids. Pudden said. "Don't forget to get your wet forty.' I said. " what's a wet forty?." He said. " when your people give you money at the window after your

THE BLOOD MODULES

Visit is over your people will give it to the officer at the window and he will dip into some water and give it to you all wet. they dip it in water just in case there is drugs taped to the money and the water will wash is off and that's your wet forty. Your only can get forty dollars one each visit."

" Jones, watch the gates, the gates are opening." the officer said. I walked to the front of the tier and I see three other bloods that has visits. We walked to the visiting room by our selves and we didn't run into any crips. I'm glad to see my girl Lisa. Her mamma brought her up here to see me and I gave her a wave, she waved back at me. I said. " Hi baby, how have you been?. I miss you so much." Lisa said. " i'm doing just fine missing you, your mamma told me how much time you got and she said hi. the police is hot on the J-Block. they are rolling up and down the streets every five minutes. the Olympic got every hood on shutdown, I was able to make some money so you can go to the store, Ru-Roger helped me." I said. " Baby face, I'll be home soon so keep that pussy hot for me. Oh before i forget, my home boy in here want to hook up wit your cousin Pete. So next time bring her. His name is Pudden and he is a cool blood I'll call and give you his name and number okay?." "okay I'll see if she want to come with me. She said. CLICK! the phone cut off. damn that thirty minutes went by fast. we're blowing kisses to each other. I waved good by and thanked her mother for

BEHIND THESE WALLS

Bringing her up here to see me. I walked to the window and got my wet forty and true enough it was wet. on the way back to the module as soon as we walked out of the visiting room there's this line of black dudes with gray jump suits on. they is all handcuffed on a four man chain. they had that crab walk. one of the officers that is escorting them said. " face the wall, stop walking and face the damn wall i said." he is yelling at me because i wanted to see these duds. But I do remember what that pig did to that Mexican guys face so I faced the wall. I said. " Blood who is this dudes?." the homie said in a very low voice, "those are crabs from their crip module forty eight hundred. you bee them crabs in their trash man suits." I had to laugh because this is something new for me to see. they do look hard core in them trash man suits. They passed to go on their visits and we continue or walk to the module. One homie said. " Blood I started to run over there and start kicking them crabs." we all started to laugh. but the officers would have beat him down with them flash lights that they are carrying."

We get back to the module and officer Mcbey was there and he is cool. he give us a lot of day room and tier time and the guys are on the tier. I'm walking towards my cell and I notice that everyone looking into cell seven. that 187 cell. I looked in and him and Yap is in there fighting over gambling. they both got blood on their faces, but it look like Yap got the best of 187. Yap is an old school b-dog. he's in his late thirties. they are going at it. 187 is much younger but old homie is hanging with him. I see Tray and he said. " you remember that argument they had the other day? will this is what it led to. one thing about this blood module we don't rat pack (many jumping on one) we go head up and there is no stomping are beating a blood like a crab we don't get down like that. and when it's over we shake hands and hug and all is good." after the fight me and Tray went to the cell to smoke some weed . I juts bought some bomb ass weed from Peter Hype. he gave me six joints for twenty dollars. one joint cost five dollars so he showed me some love. while in the cell smoking a joint, Pudden walked in and said. " ru-al did you put in a good word for me with your girl Lisa relative Pete?." " yeah, I told my girl to hook you up up with Pete. She's bool and nice looking. Her and Lisa will be waiting on my next call so she can get your name and number." I said.

it's time to go to the roof. we can bring a small pencil and money (dimes) for the phone and nothing else. I never been to the roof we will be up there for two hours, I do need some fresh air, everybody is coming to the roof. As we wait in the hallway it's about ten officers getting ready to escort us up there. walking down the long hallway I looked to the side and i can still see that blood that was left from that Mexican's guy face that happened seven days ago and no one came to clean it up. we get to the nine thousand floor and walked by ninety five hundred door and every crab in there came to the window and started talking shit to us, and we are talking shit right back and the officers are letting us do it. the officers like this type of shit because they are going to the streets after

BEHIND THESE WALLS

two years in here so they get to see and hear all the signs and language. Once on the roof it's a sunny day in L.A. there's a big ass green screen over the whole roof top. one of the homies showed me where these crips had tried to escape. They tied up some sheets and only one was able to get away. We are four stories up. two broke their ankles and weren't able to get away and the others never made it off the roof because the ones that feel was heard screaming form their fall. It's about forty pay phones on two sides of the walls. There is seven toilets, four basketball rims. This roof is big. I see tow officers walking the cat walk on the roof. there is this glass window where the officers can look everywhere on the roof. I got a nice buzz. I'm just going to ru-lax and watch the homies play some b-ball and used the phone to call Lisa.

The two hours on the roof went by fast but it was good to get that fresh air. We get back to the module and on the tier it's all kinds of trash and other stuff. Our cells have been searched and they tore our cells up. all our things are mixed up with other guys things that's in the cell up front. there's boot prints on our food and the homies photos and Tray is mad. everybody is going off with a lot cussing and yelling. one of the Mexican upstairs said. " they raided y'all cells. they was laughing at what they was doing." Pudden said " homies don't lock down. we ain't going for this disrespectful shit. these pigs is out of line. tie your cell doors to the bars and tie the back door up with some sheet this way all our cells will stay open and they can't come from the back. They

BEHIND THESE WALLS

Want to play hard ball we can act stupid too." everybody did their part. I went to lock the back door and Tray tied the cells doors so that they can't be closed. Pudden is kicking the bar of the beds. Now we got some nice size metal poles, a lot of the homies are filling big plastic bags with clean water because they are going to cut the water off once they see that we are not going to lock it down. we then cleaned up our cells and we wait on them to come. We are united as one and not going to lock it down.

An officer got on the mic and said. " ok men we're coming in and it won't be nice. we got the dogs and pepper spray." my heart is beating fast. it's about to go down, us against the pigs. Somebody could die today I hope it's not one of us. but we are ready for whatever.

Officer Mcbey got on the mic this time and called Yap and Pudden to the front of the tier. they are the older b-dogs in here. We know that they will stay firm for our cause. they talked for an hour and i can hear the dogs barking and know they have the whole bounty jail on lock down the red light is on. I walked to the front of the tier and I can see all the officers with their riot gear on and they look ready. We got our weapons and bags for our heads for when they spray that shit.

'Men if you're not in your cells in five minutes we are coming in." Everybody started yelling. "Come on in we got something for y'all. out of nowhere the Mexicans and the white guys started yelling too.

THE BLOOD MODULES

" if you spray them your going to spray us too and we don't have anything to do with this shit." Now the pigs got to change their tactics. eight hours has passed and the homies has been trying to negotiate with them on how this can stop with out anyone getting hurt.

Yap said. " blood they said that no-one will got to the hole. or will they run up in here?. They did apologize for tearing up our cell like that. but they said that we can't get no store, roof, day room, phone and ten days on juite balls. We can get our visits but they will be in the cages and we will be escorted there. no tier time and showers every other day one cell at a time. so what do y'all want to do?."

Every body is talking at the same time. Some don't want to give in to that, others want to get this over with so we can go back to our program. I'm just listening because I'll be at home in ten days, But what ever they come up with I'm going to ride with them. alot of the homies has some good points, they did fuck up our cells. two more hours has passed it's know three o'clock in the morning and i know that tow home boys got court in a few hours. we know that the officers want to end this before they start running the court line breakfast. We came to an agreement. instead of ten days we got it down to six days and meal on juite balls and we decide it would be the breakfast meal. we un-tied the doors and cells and we kept all our weapons and went into our cells.

" watch the gates are closing." the desk officer said. three senior

THE BLOOD MODULES

officers and two sergeants and four officers all walked down the tier. they know that we still have our weapons but never asked for them. they left the tier and sent in two of the mail line trustees in to clean up the tier.

I went to sleep. we only got two hours and then I woke up to this awful smell as well as the other homies. someone said. " blood y'all smell them juite balls?." I heard about them but never tasted them and I heard that they are nasty. The main line trustees brought our trays with the officer escorts. the look of it made me say I'm not eating it and the smell is real bad. I see some big ass brown beans some kind of ground beef meat. I'm glad that i only got this for breakfast. because I know that I couldn't handle this for every meal. if you go to the hole you get this meal twice a day and you get to choose which when you want the Juite Balls.

I'm looking at this ugly food and it's in two fat balls. Pudden said. " bloods, let me show y'all how to cook this shit. take them beans out Rubber Legs and clean off the grill. Tray you and ru-al make two Bongs." I said. " blood what's bongs?." Too-Chilly said. " You don't know how to make a bong?. check this out I'll show you. You wrap the toilet paper around your four fingers and make it thick so it will burn long and then you put a dab of spit on the out side so it don't come a lose. then you put a dent at the bottom, that's so the bong can breathe. and that's how you make a bong." I made it on my first try.

THE BLOOD MODULES

The shelf that is mounted on the wall has four separate compartments, I see that someone has scraped the paint off the two top ones and there is a lot of burn marks. Pudden put the bongs in the shelf. he lit one of them and the shelf is the skillet and the food started cooking and that stinking smell went away. the food is sizzling, now everyone is cooking, the whole module is smelling good. We got so much food we put some away in a plastic bag. I tasted it and it was good. it tasted like hamburger meat I ate Juite balls for the first time i know that I wouldn't have been able to eat them with out being cooked. now i wish we could have this for every meal. the homies in the other cells said. " juite balls is a high diet and full of protein meal. when it's cooked I'm eating these juite balls like they are t-bone steaks." Everyone laughed.

I got five days left. it seem like time has slowed down since we are on this lock down. Me and Pudden got called for a visit and it's Lisa and Pete. I said. " hey baby, how are you doing?. Hi Mrs. Smith. I got five days left. it's been crazy in here we are on lock down, but I'm okay." She said. " I'm doing fine Albert, everybody send their hello to you and your Mamma said Hi and she love you. I be glad when you come home Al. I got some money if you need some. the police has slowed down on coming on the J-block and people are hanging out again." "no baby I don't need any money I still got some from the last time you came. don't come up here no more since

BEHIND THESE WALLS

I'll be coming home soon. Make sure get at B-Brown to come get me Okay. Let me sat that I love you before they cut the phone off on US. I love you (BABY FACE)." I said. right as i said that it hung up. I'm sending kisses to her and her mother. I waved to them and Pete. and they was gone.

"Say Pudden did you like Pete?. I asked. he looked at me and smiled and said. "yeah, I like her style. She got my hook up so when I get to the pen she can get at me. But she's bool."

We get back to the module and it's just like it was when we left very loud. I'm looking in all the cells as I walk by and I see Yap and 187 shooting dice again. I got one more joint I'll smoke after dinner.

Today is my last day and I'm glad to be leaving. I'm laying here on my bunk and getting my thoughts together on what I'm going to do when I get out. this life that I'm living is going to put me in prison forever. I got to find a job. I didn't hear no screaming last night. dude must be gone. I know i learned a lot from the big homie Mouse and Pudden and meeting all the these new bloods and I do hope that they beat their cases. I know that I'll be seeing a lot of these bloods at a picnic or at a hood party or even in prison but i know that I'm going to get and give a lot of blood love.

" Jones get ready your going home in ten minutes" officer mcbey

BEHIND THESE WALLS

Said. it's about six o'clock. I said my good byes to the homies in this cell. "watch the gates the gates are opening" officer Mcbey said. I was told why the officers say that, because guys got fingers cut off and legs stuck in the bars and Too-Chilly had lost one of his fingers in the bars and it was his trigger finger.

I walked out and I left everything in that cell wit the homies. i only took four smokes and four matches because it's going to take about five hours top to get release. I was told to never take anything with you when you're going home. you can always get this stuff on the streets and it's a good thing so if you come back you will be greeted with that same blood love as you did when you left. plus i don't want anyone to say that ru-all took something with him from jail. I gave up all my money that i had left. As I'm walking down the tier the homies is telling me to stay out there and enjoy life and my freedom. i get to the desk and the officer gave me my green card and told me to give it to the officer when I get down stairs. before i walked out the door, I yelled down baker Row to big mouse and said. " I'm gone big homie, thank you blood." he know why I'm saying thank you. He taught me so much that I couldn't have got form anyone and other place than in that cell.

I'm walking down that big hall and following the red line that has a signed that say " RELEASE". After fifteen days they still have not cleaned up the blood off that wall and floor. i get to release and I gave the officer my green card and he said. " MR. Jones sit in that tank and I'll go get your clothes and paperwork on your release."

BEHIND THESE WALLS

I lit and cigarette. I can't wait to get out. sitting this holding tank by myself. Three hours later this officer came with my clothes. they had (trustees) pressed and washed all my clothes. they must have a dry cleaners in here because my clothes are creased up. it feels good to have my my own clothes. "Mr. Jones walk through that door and get the rest of your property." The officer said. I end up walking through two doors and the last one opened up and I was free. it's three forty eight in the morning. I see Lisa and B-Brown. I gave Lisa and big hug and kiss. Damn she smell good. I then gave B-brown a hug and then he said. " Blood, lets get the fuck out of here. I got warrants."

We're in B-Brown 1964 Thunderbird. we get on the freeway rolling. me and Lisa is sitting in the back seat hugging and kissing each other when B-Brown said. " blood we are about to run out of gas on this freeway." he pulled the over to the side. I said. " Blood why you didn't put some gas in the car before you got here?." We got out and jumped the fence and it's in a crip neighborhood. we are lucky it's early in the morning and no-one is out side. We get to the gas station and filled up the gas can that he had in his car. We put three dollars in the car and made it to the hood and B-brown dropped Lisa and I at her house and he went home I'll see him later on the J-Block. We went right to her bed room and got our sex on and this pussy is good and tight.

I have been out on the streets for ten months and know I'm back in L.A. Bounty jail for a robbery. I'm back in this hell hole and this time I'm going to prison (THE PEN) from here, no getting out this

THE BLOOD MODULE

Time. robbery with a gun I know that I'm going to get some long prison time. Me, brother Humphery, Blue and G.J., my relatives, is in this shit hole of a jail. I don't know what part of the jail they are going to but here I am putting my stuff on that yellow line again. I know the program. i'm ready to spread my butt cheeks and cough. it's about twenty five guys in here. I got on some red and black Pumas with some fat red shoe laces. I see this other blood he got on some burgendy Chuck Taylor tennis shoes, he got to be a blood wearing them colors. I gave him the nod and he gave it back to me. I don't bee any Ereckets (CRIPS) this time.

I'm getting ready to go through the assembly line and I know what is about to happen to our Jheri curl when we get sprayed with that brown stuff. I walked up to blood and said. " I'm RU-AL from Athens Park Bloods" He looked me up and down and said. " I'm Sike from the Nickerson Gardens bounty Hunters, Blood." we shook hands and we both gave up the "B" with the shake. his Jheri curl is much longer than mines. We are the same size and age. I told him what is about to happen, and he said that he is ready for anything. We get to the shower area and I don't see that big fifty five gallon drum of that spray and no sticking our arm through that window for shots and no doctors to check us for sick dick. Once in the shower I bee two white guys put their money in their shoes. I get the money and Sike's got two dudes for their money. Out of nowhere one guy said. " somebody stole my money" and then another guy guy said the same thing. So to throw them off I said the same thing too. The officer said. " I told you to watch your money that's your lost. now get

BEHIND THESE WALLS

dressed and let's move on."

I see some things has change it's not a five hour process. Me and the homie is put into line three and this line is going to ninety five hundred dorm. I said. " blood when we get up there is going to be a lot of crabs so be ready to take off on them." Walking down the hallway where that Mexican got his face smashed was the blood still on the wall. They had painted a new mural over that spot. We get to the nine thousands floor and my heart is beating fast because the the last time I was up on this floor it was full of crabs. We got to get to O.S.S. some kind of way so we can get to the blood module. "Okay men when I call your name give me your last three numbers and step inside." The officer said. Sike's name was called first and I can see in his eyes that he was nervous, Shit I am too. he got his bed roll under his arm. he looked at me and gave me a nod and I gave it back to him then my name was called. When i walked in the first thing I bee was about ten crabs standing to the side where there is a line of phones on the wall. Some of them had their shirts off and they was on swole with some twenty inch arms. they is showing their muscle to scare everyone in there. The door didn't just shut closed it was slammed close as if we are never going to get out. This big ass crab walked up on us and looked at our tennis shoes and said. I got candy and packs of cigarettes. if you want to buy and i got them." I said " no I'm cool" I see sike standing on the side. I walked over to him and said, " I got five dollars in my pocket i took it out earlier. what ever you do don't take you money out your shoe Okay. I'll get us a pack of

BEHIND THESE WALLS

Bigarettes. Blood did you bee all them crabs?." "hell yeah I seen them, them fools is on swole. we got to watch them all day and night. you checked out how they looked at our shoes?. we got to get to the blood module fast." Sike said. I never been in here before and I remember how brazy them crabs acted when I was in here the last time I was on this floor. We both walked to the back to fine us some bunks. We only found one in the middle of the dorm. We couldn't find two next to each other and we must stick together. It got to well over two hundred people in here. we agreed the we will sleep together head to toe because we are not going to separate in this death trap.

I see about eight Mexicans on one side of our bunk. two crabs walked up and the one with all the muscles said. " Do y'all want to buy some cigs." i said " yeah let me get a pack of Camels." i reached into my top pocket and pulled out the five dollars and handed to him and he gave me the smokes and some matches and they walked away. i gave one to Sike and I lit one. I needed that first smoke to calm my nerves because these crabs look like that are up to something very bad.

In here twenty minutes and i"m looking around and i bee so many blind spots. i sat back down on the bunk. the big crab came back to our bunk and said. " cuzz, where are y'all from?." I cleared my throat and said. " I'm RU-AL from Athens Park Bloods." and then Sike said. " I'm Sike from Nickerson Garden Bounty Hunters." we

THE BLOOD MODULES

didn't have no control over where the officer put us. we're here until get to see O.S.S. and then to the blood module. so now we got to find a way to get the fuck out of this death trap. surrounded by these crabs i'm getting that feeling to take off (FIGHT) first I know i'm going to get us beat down but at least we'll go out swinging. and out of nowhere that big crab pulled out this big ass knife. it's the size of a butcher knife. the police had to give them that knife. he said. "cuzz give me all your money and my smokes back." I stood up and I know what I'm about to do could get the both of us killed, i'm not about to let these crabs just rob me. Sike stood up too. this other crab said. " cuzz just give us what we asked for. you got no win in here." I looked and they have us surrounded on all sides and I can see the hate in their eyes as they are about to rob us or kill us if we do or say the wrong thing. I said I only had the five dollars." out of nowhere a crab snatched the pack of cigarettes out of my pocket and nothing i could do with that big ass knife pointed at me. they left and I can hear them laughing at us. I looked at the Mexicans that was by their bunk has left. these crabs are jacking (ROBBING) everybody in here and we just got our ass jacked. Sike look at me and said. " blood we just got jacked by some crabs. ru-al we got to get out of here. blood, we can't go to sleep in here." I said. " yeah you're right, we got to somehow get out of here. damn, blood, did you bee that knife?. it look like he pulled it out of the of the kitchen drawer. I'm no punk or fool they would have cut us up to pieces and the officers wouldn't knew what had happen to us. Just keep all

THE BLOOD MODULES

your money in your shoe. I still don't know how much i have. come on blood i'm going to try and get us out of here. you bee those officers in that wimdow?."

I notice early when we came in the big window where the two officer are sitting and suppose to be looking over the whole doom. Well we know that we would have been dead if we was counting on them to look over these two hundred plus guys. KNOCK! KNOCK!. the window opened up and this white officer and this big ass Samoan officer are setting in there, the white officer said. " what do you want?." he said that in a tone that I just stopped him from having sex. I said. " We are bloods and would like to talk to O.S.S. so we can get to the blood module." he looked at us and smile as if he know what could happen to us and then he said. " fuck no, you can't go see O.S.S. you shouldn't be be gang banging." and he slammed the window so hard i thought it was going to shatter into a million pieces in our faces. that whit officer was no joke he hate gangs or he hates bloods. the Samoan officer opened the window back up and said. " The guys in O.S.S. are not in on the weekend but I'll call forty three hundred to come get you after count." he then gave us a wink. Sike said. "blood did you bee that red neck ass white boy and how he slammed that window?." I said. " Yeah I seen that brazy ass white boy."

We got back to our bunks and I said. " blood no way we will make in overnight in here with them crabs. so our best net is to get to the blood module, but first we got to pick out the smallest crabs and fuck them up. it should be over before that big crab come with that big ass knife. So if no one come get us after count we get off on them two crabs that's our size so be ready, blood."

" It's count time men leave you bed roll on your bunks but but bring out all your personal things, if you leave it and it come up missing don't come telling me about it because I'm not going to help you." the short white pig said. The Samoan officers is standing at the door with his clip board and ink pen and said. " i want you to give me your last three numbers when i call your name. on the way back in i want two lines so step outside." everybody started walking outside. me and Sike walked out and the fresh air is crisp and the sky was clean. we're in the line close to the wall and the crips are in the other line. I notice that we are the only blacks in this line and it's to late to get in the other one. we don't know that program doing count time so we see that this is wrong. I see the big Samoan officer walking between the two lines. I didn't know he was that damn big he is much bigger than that big crab. he stopped at me and Sike and told us to come with him. we got to the front of the line and told us to give him our names. the other officer took out our green cards and gave them to the big Samoan officer. he said. " follow me". we walked into the hallway right by O.S.S. he said. "Where are y'all from?." I said. " I'm from Athens Park Bloods and this is Sike from the Nickers Garden Bounty hunters." he smiled at us and said. " I'm a B-dog from Carson Bounty Hunters and I got y'all a ride to forty three hundred blood module. I bee this all the time bloods come to the nine

THE BLOOD MODULES

thousand floor and it's packed with crabs so don't trip, i got you and do send my love to all the B-Dogs in the module. Me and sike smiled and then our escort came to take us to forty three hundred blood module.

We walked into forty three hundred blood module and it's loud as fuck. we got new bed roll and was put into the fish tank until O.S.S. see us. there is four other blood in this cell. we introduced our selves to each other. one blood said. " Did y'all come from the nine thousand floor." I said. " yeah, and some crabs jacked up for some bigarettes that we bought from them, they had this big ass butcher knife, and we tried to get out but this white officer told us we shouldn't be gang banging. but this big Samoan officer from Carson bounty Hunters got us out of there." "yeah he got us up out of there too. blood, it's full of crabs up there." Lee said from West side Piru Hood.

It's about eleven o'clock and I'm sleepy. i made up my bed and I looked around and this module is different from thirty six hundred. there is a catwalk where the officers can look into all the cells without even coming on the tier. there is no cooking shelf to cook on. i took my money out my shoe and i got one hundred and twenty dollars and Sike got about the same. we did good and if them crabs made us take off our shoes they would have came up with all this money. So the lost of five dollars is nothing.

I asked the homie Tom Slick from 456 Pomona Piru's.

BEHIND THESE WALLS

" when did they move the blood module from thirty six hundred to here?. Tom Slick said. " about seven months ago. they moved us over here because there was a riot in there bloods and the pigs. they couldn't do what they wanted to do because of the Mexicans and white dude on the upper tier. If they came in with the pepper spray it would go up to their tier. So they moved all bloods here and there are bloods on all four tiers in this module. this part of the bounty jail is called the new side. They have the crabs in forty eight hundred down the hallway. But there is still a lot of them on the main line. The only time we get to get at them is when we go to court." I said. "yeah, I was in that riot and if it wasn't for them guys on that upper tier they would have came in there and it would have got real ugly and bloody."

I was having a good night sleep when the officer flashed his light in my face and woke me and sike up for court. it was four thirty in the morning and i was sleeping good. I washed my face and put my clothes on and walked out the cell and it's about five other homies already on the tier. The tier got a lot trash on it and it's not dark like the other module. I'm going to have to get used to this module. We got the outside of the module and it's about forty guys guys going to court. in the chow hall we ate breakfast and we all walked downstairs to our court tank. Norwalk is the court tank i'm going to. I'm with two other bloods and all the others went to their court tank.

BEHIND THESE WALLS

It's about thirty guys in this chain going to court. I'm handcuffed to one of the crabs that jacked me in ninety five hundred. the homie already told me that he has the handcuffed key. The bloods has been coming out their cuffs on them crabs because they have been rat packing B-dogs on the main line. We got on the bus and the officer got off the bus to go get his paper work. I gave the homie the nod to un-cuff me. I'm in the back sike and Green from Tree Top Pirus, he got the key. all the homies going to court brought a key just for this. as soon as he un-cuffed my right handcuffed I socked that crab in the eye. he screamed like a bitch and I followed it up with two more punches and hit the floor and I started giving him the kick treatment. I said with anger. " blood where is your crab ass home boys now. What's in your pockets?." I went into his pockets and took his money and a pack of Camels cigs. the other homies came out their cuffs and beating down two crabs. they can't fight back because they still have one hand cuffed to someone else. After we was done we cuffed up to each other and then we started laughing and the crabs went to the front of the bus. they are busted up. the two officers got on the bus and the crab that I beat up said. " officer! officer I can't stay on this bus please get me off." The officer looked at his face bleeding. then out of no where the other crabs said. " us too, we can't stay on the bus either." they was busted up up too. they got the crab treatment for us. the officer said. " step up and i'll move y'all to another bus. it look like y'all got your asses kicked." everybody on the bus laughed and they was taken off the bus. the other officer said. " I'm not having

THE BLOOD MODULES

this gang banging shit on my bus."

We get back to the module and talking about the crabs we beat down. I'm back ten minutes when my name was called to go see O.S.S. and I liked the first time took my photo, answer a few question and I was out of there. And it went fast I got the ok from them that i could move into a cell. I get back and was told to get my property I'm moving to cell nine on Able row. Also came to that cell Tom Slick. Sike went to Denver row on the other side.

I went inside the cell and it's a six man cell. I'm on the top bunk. there are four other bloods already in the cell. I said. " I'm RU-AL from A.P.B." this light skinned guy said. " I'm Money Mike from F.T.B. (FRUIT TOWN BRIM)that's Too-Kool from L.A. Brims and that's Red from C.B.P. (Ceder Block Piru) and the other guy is Smooth from F.T.B.." me and Tom Slick greeted them all and started making up our beds. I started talking about my day at court the homies started laughing. Too-Kool is the oldest in this cell and he got the best bunk. The lower bunk in the back.

After I made my bed i needed to used the phone to call home. Red said. " we don't get day room time until tomorrow but you can get at one of the tier trust-Bs to make the call for you, I'm sure they would do it for you. they will be walking up and down the tier in a little while." " thank you blood." I said.

Laying on my bunk smoking a bigarette. I'm just listing on to everyone talk. They are having some good conversations. I notice the officer looking out the catwalk window into all the cells on

THE BLOOD MODULES

both sides and that's all they have to do. I can see Denver row from my cell, which is upstairs on the other side and they have four cells.

They let the trust-Bs that's what they call them in here. they are cleaning up the tier. this blood name Snoo walked up to our cell to see who just moved in. He said. " what's up blood I'm Snoo for from Family Swans." This is the homie that red said would help me and make a phone call for me. I'm said. " I'm RU-AL from A.P.B., say Snoo could you make a call for me?. I need you to call my Mom to let her know what happened in court today." " Okay ru-al I'll do it later on." he said. he had a crazy name but most gang members has nick names that sound funny but they have some kind of meaning. He stood about five foot three and about hundred twenty pounds. he got some size on him as if he been to prison. I do remember his face in the newspaper they had label him as the arcade murderer they said that he killed about five crabs and shot up many more. The homie anthony Bereal (A.B.) would always bring the newspaper on the J-block and read the B-section where they have all the crimes in L.A. Compton and Watts and we we read that and sell dope. and they had Snoo on the front page many of times. I'm sure there will be many more homies in here that I seen in that L.A. Times newspaper. Sonn came back and said. " give me the number and two dimes and what do you want me to say." I gave him the two dimes and told him. " tell my Mamma that I go to court next month and give her my booking number and to give it to Lisa so she can come visit me. and I love her." he came back with the message. he said." your

THE BLOOD MODULES

Mamma said that Lisa will be up there to see you next weekend and she loves you." "Thank you blood. Oh! do I have any home boys here?. I asked. he looked at me and said. " no one from Athens Park is here, but the home boy Big Sam from Miller Gangsta is on the other side. I'm going over there later do you want me to tell him you need a care package?." I said. "yeah, thank you blood that's good looking out."

It's my first Friday night in this module, everybody is staying up. we are drinking on some Boffee and then out of no where i hear this beat. TISS! TISS! BAM! BAM! BAM! TISS! TISS!and then this loud voice said. " IT'S SO HARD TO BE A BLOOD, It's so hard to be a B-L-O-O-D, blood. TISS! TISS!." everybody had joined in on the song and it's so loud all four tiers are singing. I can't hear myself sing. The beat is on time with the song. Too-Kool said. " that beat is from his tooth brush and his fist beating on his bunk. He took of his mattress that is why it has a loud beat." That song went on for thirty minutes or longer. It's hard to be a blood. that song is so true because bloods are out number to crabs three to one so it's hard to be a blood. It got quiet. then another beat came and the same voice said. " bloods it's roll call time. TISS! TISS! Bounty Hunters are we going to back you up?. show you right! show you right!. TISS! TISS!" he went through so many blood neighborhoods and when he got to mine "Athens Park are going to back you up?. Show you right, show you right! TISS! TISS!" we went through all the blood hoods names and there was some I never heard of but they are on the same team. this went on for four hours and now I'm

THE BLOOD MODULES

looking forward to Fridays and Saturdays. this make our hood bonds mush stronger.

I have been here for two months I'm getting close in the courts to taking a deal for the robbery. this program is not bad we just don't get any tier time, but we do get a lot of day room time. I'll take my shower today which we get every other day and then get day room time and chill and watch T.V.. I'm looking forward to my visit because I only seen Lisa once in the two months I'm happy to see her today. There are homies shooting dice in the corner and some homies playing black jack and the dice game is five dollars a bet and hand in the card game. I'm not playing because I seen what gambling can do when I was in 3600 blood module. It's a pile of money on the flood in the dice game and the homie Man Power from B.H. is shooting the dice this blood has a lot of money he one of the riches bloods in his projects. He got one of the hottest low riders in Watts it's a red and gold 1964 chevy I was told that his sound system in that car you can hear from it being parked in front of the county jail. That's bumping sounds. he got it going on and he is winning all the money.

I'm on my visit with Lisa and she look so so good. I can see the little bump in her stomach, she three month pregnant. we don't know what it's going to be but i want a boy. We had a good visit and I got my wet forty. I get back to the module telling everyone that i have a baby on the way. I'm just twenty one years old and I'm about to go to prison.

THE BLOOD MODULES

I have been going to court for the past five months and my dump truck lawyer want me to take a deal for eleven years. I told him hell, no, that's too much time. they got me as the gun man and driver so i'm going to get the most time Humphery got out. Blue took a deal for three years and G.J. got county jail time. they are going to get sentence in two week. I'm going to talk to this lawyer and see if he can get me a better deal because eleven years is just too much. I'll go to trial and get fifteen years. I'll take a deal for five to six years any more than that I'm going to trial. I know that this time is not as bad as some of the homies which some is looking at the death penalty and many are looking at life in prison. So I do have some kind of get back. it might be many years away but I'm getting out one day. Last night the homie Money Mike caught the chain to prison and he got twenty five to life so he might never get out and he's my age. Most of the homies that is fighting life in prison for killing crabs.

Being in this cell with Too-Kool I've learn alot. I listen to the Original Gangstas (O.G.) because they do have some good advice to us young bloods that want to listen I'm all ears to that wisdom and good blood values. I know that I'm going to prison and to stay safe in need all the positive information i can get and getting it from these well respected B-dog I'm all ears. I know that life behind these walls is very dangerous in so many ways.

BEHIND THESE WALLS

For the past three days Too-Kool has been talking to us young bloods in this cell about life in prison and how to conduct ourself as well as the do's and don't we need to learn all this. he's not only talking to me but I'm soaking up all I can. Some late nights i would stand at the bars in my cell and talk to China Dog from Luders Park Pirus. he's in the cell next to mines and he is also telling me how one should conduct him self in prison and dealing with other bloods things that I'm going to run into doing my prison time. I know that I talked to my big home boy Big Mouse and Pudden on how to do this time but I need more. So I said. " China Dog I know that I"m going to prison. what are the main things i must watch out for and avoid?."

He spoke low but just loud enough for me to hear every word, plus everybody else was doing their own thing. He said. " ru-al the pen is going to be way different that the streets and this module but not that much, but if you survive this mad house, prison might come easy to you. one thing you stay out of is the prison politics. politics in prison can be a very dangerous game to play and it will get ugly in an instant. also being under paperwork. Don't get me wrong ru-al being a U.B.N. or a B.L. they are still true blood solders in every way. but there can be some divisions within the blood car behind it. if you do decide to get into it, will be different than not being in any one of them. So if you can avoid that you will be okay, But no matter what they are still bloods and if they see you in a fight with a crip they will be there as you for them."

BEHIND THESE WALLS

I said. " Yeah my Big home boy Mouse has told me about the paperwork when I was in 3600 module and i decide that I'm not going to mess with it because I want to be able to love and be down to all bloods no matter what hood they are from. If they have persona beef with another B-dog I'll let them solve it and not pick sides."

It's getting late and he said. " ru-al if you get into a fight with another blood make sure it's head-up and no rat packing win or lose you got to some how make up with that person because you're going to need that B-dog someday . you don't want another blood as your enemy. ru-al, i hope this never happens, if you got to put a knife to another blood you're making a big life decision on you and your home boys from your hood and that is worse than anything because now you got hood going against each other so never let it come to that. as for them crabs you're going to run across them. they is trying to get their prison reputation just like you trying to get yours. it's going to be hard to get a head up fight from them because rat packing is their thing. You just go all out swinging and come on top if you can. ru-al let me get to bed blood your going to be okay and I can tell your a learner and I'll never tell you anything wrong and I see other O.G.s has been telling you positive shit so your going to be okay in this gang life. I said. " okay, blood good looking out."

I'm sitting on my bunk reading the L.A. times newspaper and i on the front page of the B-section and I see HUNG JURY of a mass gang killings. The guy face i had seen on the tier but never talked

THE BLOOD MODULES

to him. he's always up and down the tier. he have some long braids and if you seen him on the streets you would think he was in high school. The newspaper talked bad about him then the newspaper talked about the six hundred to seven hundred murders by gang violence in L.A. in one year. His case and a few others are facing the death penalty. I hope they get off because death row is the bottom of the prison world. But those guys seem so up beat and humble in here.

The next day me and China Man started talking again and I can see that he has taken a liking to me and I like his gangsta style. He said. " ru-al if you see a crip fighting someone out our race you got to help him because that is the one thing you must do help another black man because it could be a race thing and if you don't help it would look very bad on you and our race that another black didn't help."

I said. " yeah I understand I had a encounter like that in job corps with a crip." we talked for hours and I can tell that our talk for the day is about to end and he said. " ru-al one more thing and i want you to listen to me on this. some homies will try to get you caught up into their personal beef with another blood. make sure you go the right way on that because you could get you and your hood into some real dangerous shit. and your homies wouldn't even know what's up but they are fighting beside you. ru-al you got to watch out for the trap. some home boys words are very trustworthy and you got some that know how to get you crossed up.

THE BLOOD MODULES

I've seen the fake paperwork that was put out so other can turn on that person. The guy that is showing it to other homies so that they can turn on someone that they don't like and it turned out to be not true. and to find out the guy that is showing this paperwork had bad things on him. and if i would had reacted to that paperwork i would have been in the middle of it. and it turned out to be a lit. Homie I have seen some paperwork get typed up and it look just like it came from the courts but it was typed in his cell and he showed others and the believed it to be real and that guy got stabbed up on a lie. that is what a person would do if he want to get someone out the way. it's a lot of people that fallen for that trap and now they can't walk the mail line behind some shit like that and this was a down b-dog. so you see everything is not what is seem. So to say this young blood. anything from a third party I got to really look at their motive on why they want me to know about this. so before you just react and speak on it and put your life in their hands and on their words, think and look at the whole picture and ask questions because it's your life that could be put on the line from some fake paperwork. Well ru-al let me go for know your going to be bool blood."

After that talk I went a made a cup of boffee. I made a bong and put some water in the milk carton tied the string on the top and put the bung by the air vent so it can suck in all the smoke. but i made my bong where very little smoke come out. I found out that Newspaper is also good to make a bong it stay lit longer. I cooked my boffee and lit a smoke and got on my bunk.

THE BLOOD MODULES

After that strong shot of boffee I'm laying down thinking about what me and China Dog has been talking about over the past few days. I got to get all I can from these O.G.s because I might not get another chance to talk to good B-Dogs like them. I know that i don't want to get caught up in any bullshit. I want my reputation to be gangsta. being groomed by Big Mouse, Pudden, Too-Kool and China Dog with all them years of knowledge I know the stripes I get I got them the right way. I got some earned on the streets. now I'm on a different level. and I know that some crabs are going to earn their strips and being groomed by their big home boys. so when our worlds collide i got to be on top because my O.G.s won't have it any other way. B-Dogs on top.

I tried my hand in shooting some dice. I know that it's a no no for me but it's only for one dollar. I know I shouldn't be doing this. I'm doing good then the shit hit the fan. my cellie Smooth said. "ru-al i caught the dice you don't win, blood." He is much bigger than me and I can see the anger in his eyes. I said. " i rolled and hit my point. you got to catch the dice with your hands and now your saying you caught that with your voice so you lose, blood." I picked up the money and stuffed it into my pocket. I stood up and blood is talking alot of shit. Smooth is dark skinned and he had been in Y.A. or the pen before because he do have some size on him. he is talk some big time shit and I'm feeling threatened and when I get feeling i got to take off first. I stole on him the punch hit in thew jaw. I'm trying to end it all in one punch and I came with two more and this blood is not backing up and I'm hitting him with some solid punches. he shook it off and hit me in the nose and that backed my ass up. now i can't see shit my eyes are watery he's coming with both fist swinging at me i'm trying to block them but I can't see them coming, i got in one lucky punch and it slowed him down and then he came back in. that when the big homies stepped in and stopped the fight. they wasn't going to let him beat me down like he wanted to. I wiped my nose with my T-shirt. it's a lot of blood coming out. i feel some knots growing on my forehead. Smooth walked up to me and said. " you okay ru-al?." I said. " yeah I'm bool blood." and we hugged and shook hands and started laughing at each other. he got a little blood trickling down the corner of his left eyes. so i'm not the only one that is bleeding. my first fight with a b-dog and i lost. some of the homies started saying. " good fight but that sock in the nose slowed you down." I didn't know if my nose was broken because it wouldn't stop bleeding so Too-Kool took my t-shirt and grabbed my nose and i heard a crack sound and it hurt like hell. Too-kool said. " there you go ru-al I put your nose back in place. you got your fist broken nose. don't make this a habit hA! HA!." I had my first fight with a b-dog and I don't like the outcome. i know the next time i'm going for the nose. I learned something with that loss. I woke up this morning with two black eyes and a swollen nose. on the way to the chow hall I stopped by the phone to look at my face and I looked like a raccoon with my two black eyes. the homies said. " damn ru-al that's from one punch? he got you good."

THE BLOOD MODULES

on Able row there are some real bloods legends from their hoods so if you said their names they will be known I had the privilege to meet. Santa Klaus from N.H.B. , Gangsta Nate from W.S.P., Bro Ham from B.P.S., Man Power from B.H. Lunch Meat from P.D.L. and I'm sure there are many many more on these rows in this modules and they all earned their reputations by riding on them crabs. that is a legacy i want to leave. Big Hurk from L.P.P. is singing, he sing all the slow jams and he can sing. he put me to sleep many of nights. if you ask for a request he will sing it.

I got used to getting my roam on. some days I'll stay out my cell all day and night. I would ride right under the officers window and when everyone is locked down I would roam the tiers. i was hanging out with the trust-bs they have their own cell and get to have tier time all day. this day the officers seen me and called me to the front gate and took me straight to the hole. I told the homies in my cell that they could have all my food. I know that i'll get it when i get back.

I get to twenty one hundred on Denver row cell eleven. I walk in, the cell is so small I can stretch out my arms and touch both side of the walls. I got a top bunk cell being it's only a one man cell. I made up my bed from the bed roll they gave me. I'm standing at the bars listening to some guys talk and one said. " cuzz! you that just came in, where your from?." I know that is what we do when we want to know if your a crip or blood I know that he seen my black and red Pumas tennis shoes. I said. " I'm from Athens Park Bloods why?."

THE BLOOD MODULES

No one said anything for five long minutes and then the same voice spoke. " cuzz we got us one in cell eleven, Y'all know what to do when he pass by for showers." Why would that crab say that. now i know that they are going to try and do something to me. They are talking shit calling a slob, buster, mark and laughing. I must be the only blood on this tier. I do remember the big home boys telling me about guys that like to talk shit while their still in their cell. he called them cell soldiers. they are all mouth and it's time to get down they are the first to run and ride and they lose if they do try to fight. I'm not going to get into a talking war with them I'll just let them be a cell soldier with their home boys. When I bee them it won't be any talking I'll just take off and my action speak for me.

I got on my bunk and started reading this book a Louis L'Amour western. Somebody left in this cell. I read for about two hours and them crabs are still talking shit. I looked at the walls and seen a lot of guys that wrote their names and message on the wall. I see the homie from the streets Teddy Blow. I found this very small pencil and signed my gangsta autograph too. Pudden told me that if you write your name on the jail or prison walls you will be back to see it. I don't know how true it is but i got to sign my gangsta name in this cell. I wrote. "ru-al A.P.B. C/K all day." and then I ex out this crab's name that was there. i know that my name will get ex out someday. I wasn't able to bring any cigarettes and I'm

THE BLOOD MODULES

nicking like crazy I need to smoke. I got ten days in this hell hole and I took days of breakfast on Juite balls and i don't have any matches to cook them and this cell have the right shelf to cook on. I put the book down and went to sleep.

The guy next door didn't talk. I tried to talk to him but he never said anything back to me. For two days I watched him leave his breakfast tray on his tray slot he would never get up to get it and the officer would get it and throw it away so I started taking his tray and throwing away the Juite balls away. I did eat some of it but not all because it wasn't cooked. I did my showering in my cell I'm going to let them crabs get a free shot at stabbing me or throwing piss and shit on me when i walk by their cells. I'm not going to let them get some free shots at me and i know tat they would love to get me like that. My ten days is up and my black eyes has healed up and I'm fresh again.

Back in the module I'm happy to be back with the homies. the ten days went by fast, when I got back to my cell the home boy Cyclone had come. he only have three days and he's back on the streets. The day is going well until we started arguing with each other over some dumb shit. he swung at me and missed and went right for his nose and I missed I caught his jaw and he said. " ru-al you think your little ass can fight." He got this smile on his face as to show that he's having fun but I'm not. he put together a left right combo and caught me in the jaw and forehead. i took his punches and he came in again and I couldn't stop the three punches. I tried to grab him. what the fuck I do that for? he got me in a head lock and about to choke me out. Too-Kool seen it was going one way and he broke it up. when i got my sense back in my head i said "yeah blood you got me good this time but there will be a next time Cyclone." he said, Whenever you're ready ru-al you better put on some weight because you're a little light in the ass to hang with me. even then you'll get the same thing." We shook hands and laugh. here I am one hundred and twenty pounds and he's one hundred and eighty pounds with some eighteen inch arms and blood love to fight, well at lease I fought back. Damn I lost again. I know this much, I can take punch.

Being in the module we can't take off on crabs the way would like to so we are having fight with each other but we would shake hands after so no love lost. that was our only way to get some anger out. so going to court and coming out of cuffs, i did it the last two times I went to court.

Today I'm taking a deal for five years. My dump truck ass lawyer was able to get the District Attorney (D.A.) to break down the eleven years he wanted to give me. Being in the module for five months I have learned a lot and i enjoyed being around all the O.G.s and the new bloods.

I got up at four thirty to go to court. it's ten other B-Dogs that's going to court and I know that we want to come out them cuffs. I got the cuff key for our bus. we went to court and there wasn't any crabs to take off on. I took my deal for five years, Blue has already took his deal and should already be in the pen and G.J. got about three months left of county time. I should catch the in about four to five weeks. I told the homies that I took my deal and two other homies got life in prison. I felt bad for them because they might not ever get out but they seem to be up beat and ready to do their time.

The day room is packed today, the homies got the dice game going and the black jack cards playing on the other side of the day room. I'm not messing with either one because of the last time i got my two black eyes and a broken nose. I know that the officers can see us gambling but they are cool with it and let us do our program. I'm looking at T.V. with a few others and Smooth walks up and turned the T.V. without asking anyone. I said. " blood we are watching soul train, turn it back." He spoke with a loud voice that made everyone look in our direction and said, " so what ru-al, I'm not trying to bee them fags dance and look at them skinny ass bitches." I walked up and turned the T.V. back to soul train, Smooth spoke with a deep tone in his voice. he said. "ru-al you better turn that T.V. back to where I had or I'm going to beat your ass again." when he said that everybody is looking. they stopped shooting dice and playing cards and all eyes are on me. He got this brazy look in his eyes. my heart is beating fast and my mind is thinking all kinds of brazy thoughts. I got my ass kicked once by this dude. i never punked out before and i'm not about to start. I said. " blood you're to have to kick my ass because." BAM! i socked him in his nose he backed up. i can see his eyes getting warty, i know that feeling so i rushed him with a left and then a right and

BEHIND THESE WALLS

I connected. i got to finish him off was the thought in my mind. I came with all I had and he was taking all I'm throwing. I swung and hit him in the shoulder and I heard a pop in my thumb and when that happened he started rushing me, he hit me in the jaw and kept coming. most of his punches were missing but not by that much and I'm swinging back with one hand. I'm no match any more.. the homies notice that I was only swinging with one hand they stopped the fight by that time blood had got the best of me and once again I lost to Smooth. Just like the end of the first fight we shook hands and laughed it off. one of the homies said. Damn ru-al you can't beat blood, now you got a broke thumb but you did get down." I never lost a fight until i got in here and everyone I fought was much bigger and strong that me. I don't look at it as a loss but as a learning process that hurt like hell. This is not high school or job corps and they sure is not crabs these B-dog know how to fight and when I leave here I'm going to right there with them.

Three days later I'm looking through the catwalk over on Denver row and I can see two homies over there fighting. Me and red is talking about how they was fighting and I said. " blood they can fight." Red looked at me and said. " ru-al they can't fight, what do you know about fighting you lost your last three fights." he laughed after he said that and i said. " fuck you blood." I then socked him with my left hand because my right thumb is broken. I didn't have

BEHIND THESE WALLS

that much power but i got him good. Red got this Red hair that's how he got his name. He is a bit smaller than me. I know I can't lose this fight even if it's one hand. he came in head down and I swung and missed and was able to grab me. he wanted to wrestle. I was able to put him in a head lock and as always Too-Kool broke it up. I'm on one side of the cell and he is on the other side and at the same time we both started laughing and we hugged because we really liked each other. I said. " I didn't lose the fight even though it was short. HA! HA!." I hear a voice above me on Charlie row say. " ru-al I bee you getting ready for the pen. blood it don't matter how many fights you lose what matter your still ten toes down and when the smoke got clear you're still there. do you know who your talking to?." "nope" I answer. The voice said. " this is Lumberjack from Bounty Hunter Blood. you'll be okay i've been hearing you talking to some real gangsta down there. take their words with you blood because you already got a big heart."

I got a visit coming from Lisa today. it's been a while since i last seen her and I want to see how big our baby bump has got. She walked up with her mother. I gave her a hello and her mother waved back to me. before the phones got cut on I see Lisa don't have the happy smile on her face. " hey, baby, hi, how are you and the baby doing?." I asked. she started crying, i'm thinking something bad has happen. when i looked at her she have on this big jacket so I wasn't able to see her stomach she eight month pregnant and should be showing.

THE BLOOD MODULES

she said with a tremble in her voice. " Albert, we lost or baby, i was in a car accident. I was going to the home boy Muscles funeral when the car behind us hit us and then our car hit the one in front of us. i had pain in my stomach so i went to the hospital right away and the doctor said the baby had died from the impact of the wreck. I'm so sorry Albert." I couldn't say anything. tears running down my face. I'm in so much hurt and pain and i can see the hurt in her eyes. She said, " my relative Dwayne had killed Muscle in the Nickerson Projects he should be in the blood module with you, have you seen him?." I said. "no, he must be on the other side. Lisa when did you lose our baby boy?. with tears coming down she said. " I lost him five days ago. it was hard for me to get a visit to come see you. I'm not feeling to good and you're about to go to prison. I'll be here Albert when you get out." "baby, this is going to be a long and slow ride, i couldn't ask you to wait for me all that time. so live your life." I said. CLICK the phone went dead. I said I love you Lisa through the window and she said it as well. And they was gone.

I get back to the module and I go right to my cell. I didn't say any thing to anyone. the homies felt something was wrong because when I come from my visits I would talk about how good the visit was but not this time. I got on my bunk and I'm looking at the ceiling and tears start rolling done my face. my heart is hurting and I know that I could be leaving any day now, this could have been my last visit. Too-kool said. What's up ru-al are you okay?.

THE BLOOD MODULES

I looked at him and said. " no, Lisa lost our baby, blood." everybody in the cell said how sorry they was for me. and I felt that blood love on my feelings. it went silent and then Red said. "Blood you're going to get out someday you can make another, alot of these guys may never have any kids because they have life in prison. So help me make some bongs and we are going to drink some boffee." I smiled and said. " Okay blood, that is right alot of the homies will never get that chance, Thanks blood."

I think i will be catching the chain in a week or two. Most homie that went to the pen caught the chain one to two weeks after they got sentence. It feel good to hear the roll call tonight. it went all night. after that someone said. " get your bitch ass under the bunk, take your clothes off first and you bet not scream punk." no body is talking any more, you can hear a pin drop. I don't know whose cell that is but who ever it is he's being punked and he's not fighting back. Then someone in that cell said." blood we are going to roll up all busters. if your a buster and your home boy from your hood don't roll you up somebody will. We are going to start buster day." i still don't know who that is talking and I don't care it's not my business. I'm glad that it's not me. But they know I'm going to fight. to not fight you get put under the bunk until they let you out the cell.

The gates popped open for breakfast and ever body stepped out their cells to see who was that getting punked. I never talked to him. he only been in here for two days. he's walking down the tier with just his draws on and there are some shit stains in them. I don't know if he got fucked but to come out that cell like that something had to happen and only them guys in that cell knows. Now he got to go to the mail line and them crabs going to find out that he come out of this module they are going to eat him up unless he tell the police to put him in a P.C. cell. he's lucky that he didn't get beat up real bad. I don't know what he did to his home boys, what ever it was they had to get him out of there and he can't clam their neighborhood any more. I don't feel sad for him because he could have fought back and take the ass kicking. what just happened to him is going to last the rest of his life. losing a fight only last minutes.

Thirty minutes after dinner the loud speaker came on and someone started rapping. and the person that is rapping is disrespecting us. We started going crazy. the officer had brought a crab from forty eight hundred to rap. the officer let the crab inside their cat walked to use the mic and that crab rapped for three minutes. one minute later the officer got on the mic and said. " Who want to go down to the crip module and rap?." everybody started yelling at the same time. I can't rap so I didn't say anything.

"fuck them crabs I'll go." someone said. everybody know the right person to really dis them crabs and represent the blood module so we sent Kartoon from Bounty Hunters. Kartoon said. " blood I',, go down there and trust me they are not going to like what I got to

BEHIND THESE WALLS

Say." Fifteen minutes later blood came back and said. " blood i lit them crabs up a b-dog way. their module smells like piss and shit." the officer got back on the mic and said. " the bloods won the rap off." we went crazy with joy know he could had said the same thing to them crabs but we didn't care we sent our best and he did what he had to do give it to them crabs. out of nowhere I hear. TISS! TISS!. So hard to be a blood, it's so hard to be B-L-O-O-D blood TISS! TISS!. that went on for hours because we know that the crabs in forty eight can hear us. That beat with the tooth brush and his fist and the bunk and the beat was loud and right. I'm going to miss this when I leave.

Three o'clock in the morning the officer came to my cell and said. " Jones get ready in five minutes because your catching the chain." I got up and the other homies in the cell did as well, I'm saying my good byes to China Dog and told him thanks for the schooling and also Too-kool, I'll never forget the words I got from these O.G. bloods. Lumber Jack said. " ru-al keep your head up and stay down blood, little do you know the blood module is harder than most pens and you hung in here." I said. " okay Lumber Jack you b-up as well." I earned my respect in this module and it didn't come easy. and i did it with the utmost respect for all the other bloods.

I'm the only blood catching the chain from here and I'm nervous as hell. I'm not scares but my nerves is real jumpy. I learned to use that feeling to stay on my toes, the door closed and I'm on my way to the pen.

BEHIND THESE WALLS

Four and a half years later i walked back into the doors that sent me off to the pen, I'm not that hundred and twenty pound twenty one year old young blood. I'm now two hundred and twenty five pounds and nineteen inch arms. I'm on swole and I come back with and good prison reputation to go with my street rep. I did feel like the blood module was much harder than then the pen. Lumber Jack was right on that. We now have two blood modules 4300 and 4600 I'm going to 4600 because 4300 is full of bloods. over them three and a half years in the pen bloods and crips has been putting in work on each other. So the death rate went up and the dope cases also went up. I'm here for selling drugs so I'm going to see if I get a nice deal. Things has changed since I was last here. now they got blood hoods separated. It's not mixed up like it used to be.

I didn't have to go to O.S.S. they don't do that any more you say your a blood your going straight to the blood modules, Their is no more going to the nine thousand floor no more doctor checks. So many people are coming to jail they don't have the time and man power to do what they was doing four years ago in this county jail. now everything is fast and more dangerous and the officers are more crazy because they are getting jumped on the main line and shot up on the streets so L.A. Compton and Watts are cities that has exploded with death and violence on every block. And in this living hell hole the officers has up there madness with the beat down and other hard core moves they have to make our lives a living hell.

THE BLOOD MODULES

When I walked into 4600 it was loud. i was told to go to Denver row by the officer. I walked in and I see my Y.G. Clone and LIL Duck and Doony. I greeted them all. we are all from the Athens Park Bloods and we are in a four man cell. I hear someone call my name. " ru-al is that you up there, blood?." the voice said. and off the top I knew who it was. my brother Wayne's ex-wife son (Gary) Hands he got that nick name because his hands are really to big for his arms that held them mitts. " yeah I know who you are nephew. What's up blood? yeah this is your uncle ru-al." I said. hands said. " blood you know I was just at your Mamma's house looking for you. you know my little brother Korn is fucking your homegirl BAY-BAY. it's been a while since i last seen you uncle. My sister Shareen is doing well still living with my moms on lime street. do you need anything? if so let me know I'll get it uncle." he started talking about when I used to spend night at his house in the 1970s and they had all the cool toys. know the two boys are grown and crab riders.

Hands Yelled back up to me and said, " uncle , Zell is on this row he is on a visit when blood come back I'll let him know you're up there." I said, "Okay." Baker's row has all Pirus on their tier. on this tier has mostly Swans, Publeos and Bishops. those hoods has all the cells but this one. Swans has four cells so they are deep with home boys from their hood. Big Peanut from Swan came to my cell, he is a trust-b. I do remember him from Atkins Jheri curl shop in their hood. he said. " ru-al what's up, blood. if you need

THE BLOOD MODULES

any thing let me know, okay." I said. "okay, blood I might need you to make a phone call for me later." I'm being greeted from all these bloods some I have seen on the streets at hood parties because i went to a lot of them and I know some heard of me through word of mouth.

Just about everyone on this tier got murder cases and all of them are Y.G.s eighteen, nineteen and twenty year old and putting in work on them crabs. And that is all these Y.G.s know is to blast on them crabs. And they are running around like they don't have a worry in the world. I'm here for a dope case and i just don't know how the police know to go right to my stash in my car. I'm on Cook street with Jamala. I just knew that they wouldn't find my Rocks but they did. they let jamala go and take my car home. Somebody had to snitch on me. so the police gave my caddy to her so that was bool they didn't impound it. I was going to sex her ass up but know I'm here in the bounty jail with a bunch of hard heads.

It's four o'clock in the morning and I'm going to court. I don't remember going to court this early. it's eight of us from 4600 and five more homies from 4300. I'm hoping to take a small deal because I already got the one years violation so I'm going to see if I can get the eighteen month to two years. We ate our breakfast and was told to stand outside the chow hall. We get out there and it's ten officers out there waiting on us and they got the waist chains to cuff us up.

THE BLOOD MODULES

" Face the wall you guys know the program." one officer said. I'm thinking why are we getting handcuffed now the buses don't leave for court until six o'clock. I put my hands behind my back. one officer wrapped the chain around my waist. he then tied the two lose cuffs to the chain and then another officer came to help him. he placed one of my hands on top of the other and cuffed them up and couldn't move my hands at all. once everyone got handcuffed we got escorted to the court tanks. five of us is going to Compton court and I got two of my Y.G.s with Luna Tick and Clone. Luna Tick is housed in 4300.

" Luna Tick, why are we handcuffed like this and down here so early?. There is no one else down here". I asked. " OH! you're not knowing about this, this is called the new jack swing. They came up with this because we have been coming out our cuffs on them crabs. so to stop us they started this. and as you can bee you can't move your hands or your arms, that's the new jack swing. in about thirty minutes your hands will get numb and you will not have any feeling in your arms. HA! HA!." he started laughing. I thinking wow we started the coming out the handcuffs and this is the pay back we get for that. They must be used to it because they are laughing.

The homie Evil AL from D.L. is laying on the ground trying to get some feeling back into his shoulder, but it's not working. He said. "Blood this shit is no joke, i got to do this five times a week because I'm in trial. a lot of homies have been taking deal because of this new jack swing, Last week one homie took fifteen years to not come to court any more. they are not doing the crabs like this and they are letting them come out their cuffs on b-dogs and the pigs is letting them." I can see why the homie took that deal. this pain is no joke. I know i'm really going to go in there Monty Hall and let's make a deal, because no way i could hang with this.

We stayed in that court tank for three hours and I got no feelings in either arm. i tried everything to but nothing would work to get the blood black flowing. I can't wait to get to the courthouse and get these cuffs off. we got put on the bus and they put us in the front cages away from everyone else. and this cage is so small, it's hard for me to get comfortable. I got to find a spot and stay in it. the music is on and i can't enjoy it because of the pain i'm in. we get to the courthouse and I was so so glad. the officer said. " once you're off the bus, face the wall, you guys in these front cages your getting off first." I'm happy he said that. I'm looking at the wall and both of my shoulders are on fire and numb, he took off the first cuff my arm dropped to my side and then the other one. "wasn't you told to put your fucking hands on the wall after the cuffs come off?." the officer said. I said. "man I can't move or feel my hands and arms. I can't move them. he said. " why haven't y'all told the judge that you're being handcuffed like dogs. this shit don't make any sense to me." Evil AL said. " man we talked to the judges and they said that they was going to get this stopped but the county jail said that the courts don't run our jail. and as you can see, we are still like this."

THE BLOOD MODULES

once we got into our little holding tank i lit a smoke which I needed very bad. Luna Tick said. " We don't get handcuffed on the way back like that and I got my cuffed key just in case we be some crabs."

I get in the courtroom and I see my lawyer and i said. " i know the D.A. is offering me a deal so what is it?." He said. " he offer you sixteen months, and if you take it you can get sentence right now and catch the chain in two to three weeks. so what do you want me to do?. I said. " let's do it." I took thew deal. out of the sixteen months I'll do eight months but my parole violation will eat that up with the year I got to do off that. so I'm good on this deal and I don't have to get new jacked any more. I see why the homines took those deals. i think that these lawyers and D.A.'s know this and that's why he was quick to offer me that deal and knowing that I'm going to take it. I feel sorry for the homies that's going to trial five days a week and got to get new jacked.

Me, Luna Tick, Clone and Evil Al are on the last bus back to the bounty jail. there are four crabs on the bus. one of the crabs was talking shit to Luna Tick. the bus got on the freeway and homie gave the nod and Luna Tick got un-cuffed and then he did the rest of us. one crab said. " cuzz the slobs are coming out their cuffs." Evil AL socked one in the jaw and i started beating down the one that i'm close to. I'm putting hands on this crab. Clone is fucking up one and Luna Tick is giving one the kick treatment. I don't know how he got on the ground but he is getting the shit kicked out of him.

they are screaming like bitches and they can't fight back like they want to. they only got the one free hand and cuffed to someone else we fucking these crabs up and the officer in the passenger seat said. " Hey cut that shit out. I said stop that fighting." we are beating these filthy mack nasties down. after we stopped, the crabs, went to the front of the bus with them other guys that is hooked up to them. I know now that they are going to keep the bloods in that new jack position after this. I know that this is my last time going to court I took my deal.

We get back to the county jail and when we pulled up to the back of the jail there was fifteen to twenty officers standing out there and half of them got their big flash lights in hand and black gloves on. the officer that was driving and his partner got off the bus and started talking the officers standing there and ready for battle. I said. " look bloods there is our welcome home party, they are going to beat us down." looking out the window the two officers was done taking and the bus is quiet.

The officers made a soul train line that we are going to walk through and there will be no dancing in this line. the first crab got off a officer grabbed him and the other one hit him with that flash light. we all know that we are about to get our beat down by these pigs. I stepped off the bus and two officers grabbed and shoved me up against the wall. if i hadn't turned my face it would had got busted up like that one Mexican dude on my first time here. one of the officers said. I'm sick of you fucking gang bangers, get

THE BLOOD MODULES

your ass inside." he got me by the back of my shirt and I can't do any thing because I'm handcuffed. one of them is holding the cuffs and he started to squeezed them as tight as he can on my wrist. he shoved me into this small holding tank by myself.

I can hear a lot of screaming and yelling they are getting a beat down who ever that is doing all that screaming. I can't look out the one small window because they taped some dark paper on it. they locked the cuffs on me so tight I can't move my fingers. I'm laying on the flood so my arms don't hang down from standing. But that didn't work. I have been like this for about two hours and no-one came to check in on me they might have forgot i'm in here. Another hour has passed which seem like three hours, the door open and I'm still on the floor. The officer said. " Jones get up someone is here to take you to your module, and i hope you learned your lesson. don't be fighting on my bus."

it's four o'clock in the morning and I'm just getting in my bed. I got no dinner and the homies had woke up i see the other two homies are still downstairs. I told the homies what had happen and they laughed. Luna Tick and Clone walked in the cell and they was lumped up. they got beat down real bad. I smoked a bigarette and got back in bed because my body is in pain. I'm laying there and thinking I got to get my black ass out of this bounty jail before these pigs kill my ass. I'm glad i got my deal and on my way to the pen where the prison officers show more respect for inmates. these officers are crazy.

THE BLOOD MODULES

Today is Friday and they still having buster day going on and they have took it to a higher level. We got a buster in our cell, James. He was living in another b-dog cell and they was doing their fun thing that they do to pass the time. but James didn't want to play and they called him a buster and those are fighting words in here and he didn't want to fight either so the other bloods in that cell made him get out. Since he was not from their hood he was hands off because there is someone from his hood to handle him so he's in our cell. We got to show all the blood on this tier that we don't hide busters. Peanut came to our cell. And said. " ru-al you how we get down. you got to deal with your own homies and i told my home boy not to put hands on him." I said that's good looking out blood, much respect."

Dudes have been getting rolled up for snitching, running out on a home boy or something that happen on the streets for what ever reason you must get dealt with. I can't hear dudes screaming and I hear some Chuck Taylors tennis shoes making that noise when someone is fighting. Everyone know that sound. Now it's time to roll his ass up. I said. " Clone you want to fuck him up blood?." "Yeah big homie I'll dust his ass off. Get up James you can back if you want to, but you can't claim Athens Park any more after today. we can't have no skinny scary from hood. James you're lucky we don't have any booty bandits in this cell because you will be screaming like that buster in that other cell getting his man hood took." James got up and Clone put hands on him he never got a punch off. he didn't really fight back but he knew if he hit blood he would

THE BLOOD MODULES

he would get his ass really beat down. Clone beat his ass and told him to get under that bunk and he did, before he got under the bunk he was told to take off all his clothes and he did, that made me so mad the see this dude not fighting back or for his own manhood. he's under the bunk butt necked and we started playing some cards (spades). I still hear dude screaming and i for sure that he is getting fucked and sucking on dick. that is such an eerie sound and I know James is under the bunk scared to death but I can't help him because is I show any weakness other bloods will say that " Athens are soft." and i can't have that. he is so lucky that he got out that other cell because he could be getting fucked. I hear fights going on downstairs I know in the morning when the gates open it's going to be alot of busters coming out every cell. and it's going to be some wearing some shitty draws down the tier.

The gates got racked for breakfast and I stepped out and James walked out whit his head down in shame, he got lumps everywhere, there are busters walking down the tier looking like the elephant man with big lumps and the dude that was doing all that screaming he's walking down the tier with nothing on not one stitch of clothes on. We let our buster put his close and keep his shoes. we treated him bad but not as bad as the others did their busters. we know that he is going to the main line and we hope when he run into them crabs he fight back. we even let him keep his shoes.

It's about about six busters at the front gate on our tier, I know that every tier is sending their busters to the front gate. all

THE BLOOD MODULES

together sixteen buster got rolled up in 4600 this day. not counting the ones in 4300 module. The officers know what time it is and they don't say anything. they let them all out first off every tier and they are going to place them somewhere on the main line to protect them because most of them will get ate up out there on the mail line. I catch the chain.

I'm only on the streets for forty five days, the shortest days I ever been out and know I'm back in the blood module and I'm going to take the first deal I can get and i did sixteen months and as the last two times my Violation will eat that up. I'm glad that the courts stopped the county jail from that killer handcuff the new jack swing. As always I'm welcomed with open arms and a lot of blood love. We are still having buster week. out only forty five day Mamma has been saying that this jail and prison is my second home. I think she feel good sometimes when I'm locked up because she knows that I'm going to be safe. it seem like every time I come to jail someone in our hood that everyone knows got killed so being in prison Mamma was at ease because it could easy be me from the things I was doing out there. and i could be 10 toez down (dead). but somehow I'm in here where i know how to handle myself.

L.A. bounty jail is more dangerous than most prison main line. The homie Lumber Jack wasn't lying when he said that if you can hang in here you can hang in any prison. it's more rules political rules in all prisons and for all gangs and non-gang members. and the guards

THE BLOOD MODULES

in most prisons do show a lot more respect. and the Bounty jail officers had to play their hard core role because they was going to the streets and couldn't show no weakness in front of their working colleague so they are pushing their line and we as gang members are pushing our lines. And when they hit the streets they are going to take all that anger with them from out this county jail. it will be a graduation for them too. I got groomed by some real bloods and I learned how to carry myself behind these walls I was able to pass some off to me Y.G.s and others and they listen to me. I'm not a shot caller just a down blood and keeping it real. These walls hold so many secrets and for the week you will be be preyed on and the busters will get rolled up. I know this much. from my fist time in 3600 blood module in 1984 to going through 4300 and 4600 blood modules the last time in 1990. with in those four years in that hell hole of a place i don't wish it on anyone because I'm an O.G. now i say don't gang bang or do any crimes because this place will test your mental and physical being to the max. L.A. Bounty has changed so many people lives and when they made these blood and crip modules they created something that would take a life time to fix the harm they did to human life BEHIND THESE WALLS.

CHAPTER THREE

(PRISON LIFE)

Sitting in the prison holding tank. I'm smoking my last cigarette. I don't see any crips, it's two white guys and two Mexicans and one other black guy and he don't seem to a gang member. I got on the clothes that I came in here in and they are tight, the pants are hugging my ass and the shirt is real tight. being in the blood module for six months I put on some weight. it is cold down here. I'm not that nervous being this is my first time going to prison. maybe the nerve thing will get worst once I get there. We ate breakfast very early and we was the only ones in the chow hall. So no-one is coming down for court yet. I remember what the O.G.s said, if i do it right i will be okay and they all said that I will be okay and i believe them. I'm going to be a thinker.

I hear the sound of someone dragging some chains. that's a sign that we are about to leave. two officers walked up to the holding tank they both have on these black gloves on. one officer put the chains in one pile on the floor. so this is what they mean when they say "catching the chain". The tall officer said. " okay men i'll call your name and you give me your last three numbers, then you step out and stand on this side of the wall. bring out all your property that you're taking with you." The first two guys got called before me. It's my turn. i walk up to the officer, he looked at my green card and then at me to make sure that I'm the right guy. I an glad that I'm not going first. i can look at the others

PRISON LIFE

that's in front and follow them. i don't want to be the one that fuck and get my ass kicked before i leave this hell hole.

Everyone is in line to get handcuffed. the officer said, " when i ask you to come up you will be cuffed-up and ankle cuffed and then you get back into line. do everyone understand?." "yes sir." we answer at the same time. I'm standing in line with waist chains on and my thumb is hurting, he put the cuffs on too tight i'm going to see if i can get him to loosen them up some. "officer can you loosen up this one cuff on my right hand. i think my thumb is broken broken and the cuff is on too tight." I asked. he said. " let me see, Oh! yeah i see that it's swollen i will loosen it some for you. I can't loosen it up too much. it's not a long ride to Chino prison, it's about forty five minutes from here, you'll be okay plus we're going on a bus that has soft cushion seats. Walking through booking front and out the door the air is crisp. it look like it's going to be a beautiful day in L.A. but my day is going to be gloomy. before i step on the bus the officer did one more name and face check. I stepped on the bus and these ankle cuffs is rubbing the back of my ankles and they are starting to hurt. i got to take baby steps from here on out. once on the bus I got a seat by the window so i can get my last look at my freedom.

The bus driver turned on the radio, that was cool of him. but i know that it won't stop my mind from running wild. am i going to take off on the first crab i see. or do i set back and wait?. I got i got so many thoughts going through my mind, i'll just let it all come to me and then i'll react. damn i need a smoke to calm my nerves down. looking out the window and seeing everybody doing their own thing and none of them people don't ever know what I'm about to encounter. the radio said six fifteen a.m. we should be there soon. I see a sign that says. " Chino prison next right." out of nowhere my heart starts beating fast. i can see my shirt moving from each heart beat. i got to calm my ass down, take a deep breath ru-al. AHHHHHH!, yeah that's better.

January 6 1986 the bus pulled up to the gates of Chino prison. it stopped between these two big gates and the officers got off. one has what look like a M-16 rifle. he then took the officer's hand gun which is a cannon 357. he took them into this office. when he returned to the bus and the gates opened, the bus pulled in and stopped. the gate closed and both officers got off. a prison guard got on the bus. he wore all green with a green baseball style cap. on the cap was a start that said. " California Department Of Corrections." his his shirt had the same patch on it. the guard walked down the aisle counting everybody. he went to the back, opened up the restroom door and looked in and slammed it shut, he came back to the front and got off. the two L.A. county officers got back on the and drove through the two big gates. i'm looking out the window at these guys that got on blue pants and blue shirts. they are raking up leaves and doing their thing. we pulled up in front this building and stopped. the officer got off and

PRISON LIFE

walked into the office and came back ten minutes later.

" okay, men. this is your home now. when the officer calls your name step off the bus and walk to the side and then the corrections officer will tell you what to do next. I'' be taking off your cuffs as you get off the bus."

it felt good to get these cuffs off. my thumb is throbbing and my ankles are sore from them damn cuffs. standing there next to the bus, one officer said. " men your at chino Central (R&R) Receive and Release. I'll walk up to you and ask you your name and it should match this on the card. once we're done, you see that door over there? it will open. stay in the line and then we can start the process."

" Hey, bitch!" a voice came from the building we stood by. "Yeah, I'm talking to you, with the long hair. i want to fuck you and make you my bitch." it's the same voice. I looked to where i heard the voice come from but i don't see nobody. I see the windows busted out and the building got this ugly yellow brown color. whoever those guys are they can see us but we can't see them.

"hey, you with them tight ass pants on let me squeeze your ass cheeks. I'm going to enjoy your black ass when you come in here." the voice said.

When I heard that i wanted to disappear because i know that they are talking about me. my heart is racing now and my head is getting tight. " come on ru-al get your self together, you just came out the blood module. the homies will be real upset if you punk the game now." I said to myself.

PRISON LIFE

I looked up at that window and gave them the fuck you finger and then gave up my hood and big ass "P". I'm not a buster and i'm not about to start. i got my nerves back in check. someone said. "yeah punk hold up that finger when you get your black ass in here. no-one can save you once you get in this cell HA! HA! HA!."

Standing in line i got my mind made up. anybody walk up on me and say that they seen me on the bus I'm going to sock them right in the nose, because they already told me what they wanted to do to me. and i'm not having that shit and that's on blood.

They are still yelling out the window, then the officer said. " okay men walk through that door and no talking to my workers. if i catch you it will take you longer to get this process out of the way, so it's up to you on how long you want to be down here."

once inside we are placed in this holding tank. i got my things from the county jail. i got in my property a watch and two earrings. across from the holding tank is a inmate worker. he's sitting at this desk. he said. " i got cigarettes for sale, you can't keep none of that stuff you got so if you want to trade it let me know before the officer comes back."

I said. " i got two earrings and this watch. what can i get for them?." he said. " toss them over here. i'll give you five cigarettes, but you got to wait until you're back to eat you lunch." I said. "okay." I don't need this jewelry they are cheap any way.

this inmate walked up to the bars with and pad and ink pen in his hand and asked us our clothes size, and shoe size. sitting here for an hour and this big black officer came and opened up the holding tank door and said. " men, first let get this out the way. when you address me or any other officers you can call us C/Os and the last name you see on my shirt and if you can't see the name just C/O will be fine. ou will get respect from us and we want the same but if you want to act a fool we can do that also. do i make myself clear?." "yes" everyone said. " now i put a paper bag in front of you and this trash can right here. in the bag you put the things that you want to send home and you will pay for it to get sent out so if you don't have any money to send it home toss it in the trash can. i'll be back in five minutes and i want everyone in just there draws. and everything in that bag or trash can. if you're sending something out ask my worked for a slip for your home address. do you understand?." he said. everyone said. "yes."

I'm done. i threw away all my stuff. now some of the guys want to trade their stuff but it's too late the dude is gone. only me and two other guys got cigarettes coming and i'm not giving any of mine away.

The c/o came back. this is a big ass man. he stood six foot five and tow hundred and fifty pounds and all muscles. i thought my pops had a deep voice. his is real deep. he said. " the men that is sending their things home put your bag on the bench and get back in place, everybody stand up and take off your draws and put them in

BEHIND THESE WALLS

The trash can. I'm sure everyone's been through this, so lets do it and get it over with. lift up your arms, now show the bottom of your feet, if you got dentures take them out and show them to me, and open up your mouth. okay now squat and cough three times, lift up your ball, all right now skin those dicks back."

I'm looking around because I don't know what he mean by that, skin your dick back. I looked and notice two guys pulling back the foreskin on their dick. so i did it in time before he got to me. i never had to do this in the county jail. i can see someone hiding something in their it won't be much.

Sitting on this cold ass bench necked waiting on the worker to bring me my clothes. He finally comes and i put mine on and they fit just right. i got a big size because of the weight I put on in the county jail. I won't be in prison with some tight ass clothes on and for them dudes that was talking shit through that window i'll be ready for them.

Now that I'm dressed in my prison blues, this short c/o came in and spoke. " quiet please!. i need everyone to listen because i'm only going to say this one time. these are the things that's going to happen. it can go fast or you can be here all day. i know at three o'clock i'm going home, and you will be here. okay line up, you will get wrist bands cut off and then walk to that camera and get your picture taken. while you're there you will be given your prison c.d.c number. when you get it remember it because you're a

BEHIND THESE WALLS

Number now. everything you do will have something to do with that number. after that go to the x-ray machine, then you're going to get two shots and then your blood draw. you will get one tetanus shot and T.B. shots and then you walk to the doctor and tell him about anything that's bothering you and medications you're taking. then you will be given your bed roll and fish kit. after all that you should be ready to go to a cell. and if everything goes well you'll be ready for dinner in the chow hall because i know you don't want to eat in here. so let's go."
I took my photo and i put on my mean look since that's the picture i'm going to be carrying around. I was given my c.d.c. number, D-21152. When i seen it i had to laugh because i'm in here for a 211 so this number be easy to remember. I walked to where there are two nurses and they got these trays full of needles and she got one in her hand waiting on me. she gave me a shot in my forearm and it left a little bump. I said. " why do I have this bump. I never had a shot that left a bump so i got to know what did she put in me. she said. " it will go away in two days and the nurse will come look at your arm to see if you got T.B. if you do, that bump will get big and spread. Now hold up your shirt so i can give you your tetanus shot." she picked up this gun looking thing and shot me in my back arm. I walked over to the other Lady and she took two vales of blood. I hate needles and I was making alot of noises. i walked to this doctor that's sitting behind this desk. I handed him my paperwork.

BEHIND THESE WALLS

" Hi MR. Jones how are you doing today?." he asked. I said. I'm okay." " so tell me do you have any problems i need to know about?. are you any medications?. The Doctor asked. I said." no I'm not on any medications but i do have a problem with my thumb, i think It's broken." he said. Let me see you hand, oh yes it's broken how did you break it? and how long has it been like this?." I said. " i had a fight and hit him the wrong way and it happen like two weeks ago. I also got hit in the nose and I think it got broke also but this guy i think fixed it but i want you to look at it." he said. " lean over and let me see your nose. yes it was broken but it's in place. it's going to take some tine for it to heal. So MR. Jones did you win the fight?. I looked at him and smiled and then said. " no I lost two fights to the same guy and the nose and the thumb happen at different times." Well Mr. Jones i'll get you to the doctor who will get your thumb put in a cast. it's going to take a few days for your paperwork to go through. I see that you have five years. you might get sent to west yard and if so you will get a pink piece of paper called a ducat. show it to the c/o and he will tell you where the doctor's office is. if that's it Mr. Jones, take this paperwork to that desk." he said.

I walked to the desk and this pretty looking c/o officer is behind the desk. she got long blond hair and she's short she is not bad a bad looking white lady. she said, " Mr. Jones I'm going to ask you a few questions and i need you to answer them as best you can.

BEHIND THESE WALLS

Are you in a gang, if so what's the gang name?." I said. "Athens Park Bloods," "what is your religious belief?." she asked. I said. " I'm a Christian." " how many brothers and sisters do you have?. are both of your parents alive, and do you have any kids?." she asked. I said. " I have four brothers and four sisters, and yes both of my parents are alive. no i don't have any kids." That was the hardest question to answer knowing that Lisa just lost our son so that brought back some pain. the officer said. " okay Mr. Jones you and go back to the holding tank. Lunch time will be in a few minutes." I said. "thank you." this assembly line was different from the county jail. I'm back in the holding tank. i was the third person in so the other guys got to get done before we get our lunch.

Everybody is back and the worker brought us our lunches. it's a bag lunch two pieces of bologna, four slices of wheat bread, two cookies and a apple. I tried to get two lunches but no luck. i see that the worker is back at his desk. I said. " hey bro, do you have them smokes?." he said. " yeah, hold up i'm going to throw yours and the other two guys at the same time." he tossed them through the bars in some toilet paper. i picked them up and took mine out and gave the rest to the other guys. and they are roller up cigarettes. i was looking for some camels. i gave one to the brother since he don't bang. i got my smoke on and i needed that bad.

PRISON LIFE

I'm in all blue and I don't feel good wearing all this blue. the last time i had on all this blue is when daddy bought me my first suit and at that time I didn't know anything about gang banging was. and that was a clean ass suit but now i'm in blue for some years to come. everyone is done with their check ups. i notice that these officers do show us more respect than them crazy ass pigs in L.A. county jail.

A different officer came to the bars and said. "men when I call your name give me your c.d.c. number, step up and I'll give you your house name and number. Jones step up." I said. " D-21152." damn I never been called first for any thing in my life and now i'm first in line. everyone is in line and we walked out these doors and into the hallway and i see all kinds of guys walking around freely. we was told to sit down against the wall.

" Okay men i got your I.D. cards you take this everywhere you go and when a c/o asks you for it you must have it. if you lose it you go to the office and let them know and they will make you another one but if you lose two then you will have to pay for it. and don't worry the sate has it ways to get their money. the c/o said.

Mr. Jones D-21152, your going to Cypress, cell eighteen. on the third tier. He said. Still sitting down i can see all the signs saying all the cells names. I notice that all the housing is name after trees. once everyone got their house and cells the c/o said.

PRISON LIFE

" you got your cells. all you got to do is follow the names and once you go inside there will be an officer at a desk and he will tell you where to go. make sure you show him you I.D. card.

I walked in to this open door and this officer was sitting at this desk and said. " give me your I.D. card. okay you walk up them stairs and your is down the tier. dinner time is in about an hour." I took my fort step on my way to the third tier and this is like a module but it's five tiers high. I'm thinking to myself that I'm about to really start my prison life, i thought is has started when we came through them big gates but it's now. I hear some guys talking and i smell cigarette smoke. I need to smoke me one. my nerves has raised up some. as i'm walking i get to the second tier i can look out the broken windows. i can see alot of parked cars. this is not the building that them dudes was yelling from. I get to the third tier. walking down the tier this dude said. " Where you from." I didn't say anything i kept walking. when someone ask you that question your suppose to give an answer right then and there but i didn't. I get pass two more cells and this other guys said. " say man, where you from?." I stopped in front of his cell, i looked in and he wasn't that big buy his cellie got some size on him, so I said. " I'm ru-al from Athens Park Bloods in Compton." I said it loud enough so that the first guy that asked me can hear also. i walked off to my cell and i hear one of them say. " we got us one on the tier Cuzz." this other voice said. " a what Cuzz." he answer

PRISON LIFE

"a blood from Athens Park.: it got real quiet, i'm now standing in front of cell eighteen. i looked in and i see this guy, he's little smaller than me but looks much older. I know he heard us on the tier and if he's a crab i'm not going to do too much talking. especially with my broken thumb. the cell door opened and I walked in. i put my things on the bunk and said " what's up bor, i'm ru-al." and i stuck my hand out, he shook my hand and said. " I'm Jim i live in San Diego, and i don't gang bang, I heard them guys on the tier talking to you." I made up my bed. this cell is small for two people to be off their bunks at the same time. Jim is on the bottom bunk which is cool with me. up here i can look out the window and see all the cars coming and going. I'm sure it gets cold in here at night with all the windows busted out, i might have to get another blanket. Jim let me sit on the foot of his bed, i lit my cigarette. i see he got a box of tobacco and he rolled him up one. he said. " so ru-al how much time do you have?. i only have two years and i have been in this cell for four days." I said. " i got five years." " Say ru-al, you're a blood you got alot of home boys in Palm Hall and Sycamore in this building. there's only Crips in here. there are four on this tier, most of them are on the first tier. and that's where they put all shot callers and hard core Mexicans powerful white guys. this is like their hole until they leave to a prison that they are going to do their time. You'll really hear all of them talking tonight. I do live in a blood neighborhood in San Diego." he said.

102

BEHIND THESE WALLS

I smiled when he said that and kept talking about the guys that live there and the streets and he asked me " have you ever heard of Lincoln Park Bloods?. " Naw, Jim i didn't know that there are bloods in San Diego." I said. Jim said. " yeah and there are some Sky Line Pirus and 59 Brims. You might not be here too long if you go to west yard. you will like it a lot. it's dorms and there are some bloods over there."

It's chow time and all the gates got racked (open) at the same time and i walked out first because i don't them crips to rush me in this small ass cell so I'm on the tier where i can get down and fight them. I know that they are going to rat pack me. i remember what the big homie Mouse said about guys that like to be cell soldiers. "ru-al don't be a cell soldier. when someone is wolfing behind these bars he is a buster and he can't fight. so keep calm and if that person walk up on you swing first and don't stop." so i'm going to let the gate be the bell and the bell has rung.

I do know that they said that they got them one, so i'm ready. i see one of them dudes that asked me where i'm from, the small one, and then his cellie came out and he is as big as I thought. they all got together and are talking. i wonder are they talking about me?. Jim started walking and i followed, if something should happen I don't expect Jim to help. as we're walking towards them my heart started beating faster and faster, but i'm focused. if the they rat me i got to get one of them on the bottom with me, and if they try

BEHIND THESE WALLS

To throw me over the tieri'll have one with me and i hope to be on top so he can break my fall because there is nothing but three long poles that is between us and the floor and that long drop of this tier.

"What's up bro? I'm Tone." The big Crip dude said. I spoke with no fear in my voice. "nothing much, i'm ru-al." this crab is on swole close up. he said. " we are not tripping up here, all your home boys are in Palm Hall and Sycamore, you might see some of them on your way to the chow hall." I said. "okay." none of the other crips said anything. i notice one of them had this look like he wanted to do something but his big homie won't approve. i walked on to catch up with Jim because he had kept on walking.

Me and Jim sat at the table together, dinner was good, it's much better than the county jail food. i ate a half of chicken, whole bake potato, mixed veggies, two pieces of bread and juice. and the best thing was i didn't have to rush and wolf my food down. i took my time. i'm looking at all the faces and seeing who is eating with who. Jim Said. " in the morning we got cinnamon rolls and they are as big as the tray. you will see in the morning."

" Say Jim could i roll up a smoke when we get back?. i don't have any money to pay for it. I asked. he said. " you can get a box from the desk, they give us this shit for free, all you got t do is ask the c/o. i do have a few extra boxes. They call that tobacco Deukmejian, after the sate governor because it's free and it's

BEHIND THESE WALLS

Rough on your throat, but it's good to smoke." Jim said.

I didn't see any home boys while i was in the chow hall. i stopped at the desk and asked the c/o for a box of tobacco he gave me one box. sitting in the cell I'm rolling up cigarettes. laying on my bunk listing to them crips talk and every three words they are saying cuzz as if they want me to hear them. I'm not going to trip because they had their chance to get me if that's what they wanted to do. But these are just words and their words. They stopped talking and i hear these two guys calling out numbers, they are playing chess. I said. " Jim why are they yelling out the moves like that?." He answer. " they are playing in different cells and they have their boards marked with numbers so they can keep track of their moves." looking up at the celling thinking about what's ahead for me now that i've started my prison life. so far everything has been okay. but i know that this is just the beginning and it will get worse before it gets better. all i got to do is keep the big homies words in my mind and i'll be okay. 1988 is when i touch down, damn that's a long time away.

I'm up early, i washed my face and brushed my teeth, i put some water on my hair so i can comb it. i got to do that because my hair is real nappy. I had cut the Jheri curl out three months ago and know I have this small afro. I'm hoping that i can comb it with this small as comb. nope i can't use this comb. it's too small. I lit a smoke, Jim is still knocked out, asleep, i can't hear no-one.

BEHIND THESE WALLS

I wonder what time it is. it's still dark outside so it early. There is no books in here to read but this Bible they gave me in my fish kit. I open it up and it to Psalm 118:24. After i read that, verse I thought to myself, should i be glad?. or should I be mad?. i pounder with that verse for some time then Jim woke up. But I am glad to be alive and see another day.

Breakfast time now let me see what Jim was talking about with these cinnamon rolls. I got my tray and i couldn't believe my eyes. damn they are so big he wasn't lying. i spread the peanut butter on it and it melted. that was good. on the way out i notice this black dude with his pants rolled up to his ankles and his shirt tied around his waist. and he is walking like a girl. I said. " Jim look at that fag right there. " he said. " yeah ru-al they got a spot just for them in Birch hall. and lot of guys try to get in there with all them Homosexuals so they can fuck them. Don't he look just like a women?." I said. " yeah, he do like a girl. i can't mess with them my big home boys told me about them gat dudes. but that is a pretty man though."

On my way back to the cell the c/o said. " Mr. Jones, pack your things your going to west yard, so in fifteen minutes i'll open up your and you come down to this desk okay?." I said. "okay."

Wow only here one day and I"m going to west yard. i got what little I had rolled up in a blanket and I'm ready to go. I'm going to leave the thick blanket and one sheet with Jim this should help him stay warm at night. the gate open and I said my good bye to Jim and the gate closed behind me. I get to the desk and there are six other guys with all their stuff under their arms.

The c/o said. " men line up in the hallway by the wall the way you came in. we're going to west yard and I want you to walk through that door and there you will see a van parked with it's doors open." We get out side and it's the white van. we got in it we then drove the same way that we came into the prison. in five minutes we are on west yard. the van parked in front of this small building and on the door it said R&R. everybody got out the van and was told to walk into this small room that has six long benches. I hope that he don't say get nuts to butt like in L.A. county jail. he didn't and we all sat down. I lit a smoke. a c/o came in and said. " I got your new housing and you will be here until you're called to leave to go to the prison where you're going to do your time." As the last time my name was called first. he said. " Mr. Jones you're going to Elm dorm, when your get there walk to the middle of the dorm and there will be your dorm officer. he is waiting on you so walk down that pathway and you will see the name of your dorm above the door. on your way grab yourself a fresh bed roll."

I'm walking on the pavement. i see guys in pairs walking together and there is a baseball game going. the sun feels good on my skin, being in the module for six months and no real sun light this is good. I see the weight pile on the other side of the yard. i get to

PRISON LIFE

Elm dorm and there are about five dudes standing in the front door and the door is hanging on one hinge.

" Excuse bro I'm in this dorm." i said. this tall dude spoke. " where are you from, and are you in this dorm?." My heart started beating fast. i know i'll get my ass kicked but I'm going down swinging if they try to rush me. I know that they are crips. one of them got a blue rag in his top pocket. i took a deep breath, one that no-one could see me take, and looked up at the sign that said Elm dorm and I said. " yeah I'm sure this is my dorm, and I'm from Athens Park bloods." The same dude that asked the first question said. " okay little man, you got heart. You got some home boys in Fern dorm, do you know Big Mike?." "no i don't know him." I answer. he said. " he's on the weight pile right know he will tell you about the program. we are not up here gang banging, so welcome to the dorm." 'thank you for the info i'll get at him later on I got to see the c/o and make up my bed first." I said. as i walked away my heart is beating normal again.

Walking down the aisle i see a lot of bunk beds with lockers in front of each one. every bed is made up. the floor is shinny, i don't see no other inmate in the dorm. i get to the officer and there's a c/o sitting behind a desk. he looked up and said. " you must be Mr. Jones." I said" yes i am." " this is you dorm everyone in here gets along, you will get your respect and i expect you to give it back. that is what keeps this dorm in harmony. You're not

PRISON LIFE

Allow in other dorms and your home boys are not allowed in here. you're in bed forty eight, the top bunk. you have a locker and this is your lock which you will give back to this office before you leave this dorm. your bed is to be made every morning, no one is allowed back in the dorm after breakfast unless you're helping in the cleaning, 10:00am the dorm is open to do as you please. the shower is always open. the T.V. room is also open at that time. four o'clock is count time and I want you on your bunk for that count. We go to the chow hall by dorms and after dinner you can do as you like, the yard is over at nine o'clock and count is at ten o'clock. on Saturdays they show movies in the gym and on the weekends you can stay up as long as you want to. now that you know the program do you have any questions?." the c/o said. I said. " no sir."

i made up my bed and put what little stuff I had in my locker. I walked outside and them Crips are gone but the first person I see is Blue. I said. " what's up relative?." he got a big ass smile on his face and said. " hey ru-al, i seen you coming in, i was on the weight pile. So how much time did you get?." I got five years. man, i didn't understand why i didn't see you after we got arrested, my lawyer told me how much time everyone got they was trying to give me eleven years." I said. blue said. " i'm in oak dorm and i've been there for two months and i should be leaving any day now. let's take a walk. I'll show you where your home boys are."
I have not seen Blue in a long time and he got a little size on him from lifting weights. before they split our cases up they would

us the Jones boys. we all had the same last name. and from growing up together in Watts, now in prison together.

While walking the track, Blue is telling me about the yard and where everyone hangs out. I said. Blue, where are my home boys?." he said. " they hang out on the other side of the yard. I'll take you to them after we bust a few more laps around the track, i want to kick it with my relative before i go."

Walking by the weight pile i see big ass dudes and some big Mexicans and white guys. they all are on swole, the black guys are the biggest. i got to get my thumb fixed so I can get my buff on. walking and talking to Blue has made things much better. my nerves are not jumpy any more. Blue said. "there are your home boys, I'll let you kick it with them but we will get back together after dinner." I gave him a hug and said. "okay."

I walked over to where there are three guys sitting on a table by the dorm. I said. " what's up bloods, I'm ru-al from A.P.B.." This huge light skinned brotha stood up and said. " I'm big Mike from I.F.G. this is Sta-Soft from Lincoln Park Blood in San Diego and boe from Twenty Outlaws." I said. " what's up?." I shook their hands. I'm happy to be around some b-dogs. big Mike Said. " How much do you have ru-al and what dorm your in/ after dinner we will have a care package for you because i know that you don't have anything, so meet us right here after dinner." i said. " I got five years and I'm in Elm dorm." " It's bool in there them crips don't want any problems. we lift weights in the morning so you can get

PRISON LIFE

Down with us. It look like you can use some muscles." I look at him and the other homies they got some yokes on them but Big Mike is real big. he got some twenty inch arms and a wide ass chest. I said. " I can't lift any weight i got a broken thumb. I should be going to the doctor and day and getting a cast put on it." we talked for awhile. Sta-Soft said. " Who was that dude that you was walking with? i seen him walking the yard with other crips?." I said. " that's my relative. We're here on the same case. he got three years on this case."

I see Blue walking the track with some of his crips homies, Blue that crip walk and his pants are sagging real hard. He looked at me and gave me a nod and he broke way from his home boys. I said to my homies. " Blood I'll get back, I'm going to spend some time with my relative because he is leaving any day now. " Big Mike said. " Okay go kick it with your folks, blood we will be right here and I'll have that care package ready for you."

We walked the track about seven times, Blue is saying hi to all the crips that is walking by us. there was two crips walking behind us. one said out loud. " what was your SLOB temperature?." The other guy said. " I don't remember but the took my slob in those two tubes, I hate needles but I know that it's very high."

Once they turned off the track i asked Blue. " what do that word SLOB means?." He said. " That's what we crips call bloods, like Y'all call us that "C" word." now i know what they call us when

BEHIND THESE WALLS

They want to disrespect us like we say crabs. We stopped and sat on the bench and started to reminisce when we was kids growing up on 117 street in Watts. we played as kid and we had a lot of fun times. I said. " just think if our family wouldn't moved to Portland Oregan in 1976 i would have been a crip like you." he smiled and said. " yeah, you Paul and Katie are the only bloods in the family. Now we're in prison and you're a blood and i"m a crip and there is never any love lost." " you got that right." I said.

I went to go kick it with my homies and he caught up with his. I enjoyed that time with my relative. I see the homies chillen on that same bench. Big Mike said. " ru-al we are going to the movies this weekend. when you get in the gym and you don't see us, stand in the back by the door because we always sit in the back close to the door for safety." "okay." I answer.

Big Mike handed me my care package. two tubes of tooth paste two bars of soap, wash cloth, shower shoes, tooth brush, deodorant, lotion and a lot of food. i was happy to get that blood love from them. i put all my things in my locker and went to the day room to look at some T.V. i sat in the back and the crips got control over the T.V..

I had a talk with Sta-Soft earlier about the crips and he said. " we are at peace with them. they give us our respect and we give it back to them. homie i know that you just come out the blood module and that's how y'all got down on them crips but you will see that prison is different from the streets and the county jail. it's just

BEHIND THESE WALLS

A little bit more respect. I know that you come to ride on some crips who knows you might get that chance. don't rush it, you don't get out until 1988." I said. " I hear you good looking out blood."

Last night I got my ducat to go see the doctor for my thumb. I walked to R&R where the white van is waiting on me. I got in and i wasn't even handcuffed. That felt good. it took us less than five minutes to pull up in front of the doctor's office. I walked in with the one officer by my side, I sat down and this inmate worked came from behind this door and said. " Mr. Jones let me have your I.D. card and come with me so I can set everything up for the doctor." i followed him into this room and sat on the bed that they have. now the doctor walked in and said. " Okay Mr. Jones, so you got a broken thumb, let me see Ah yes, i can feel it. Okay this is what i'm going to do. I'm going to numb it first and then push the bone so that it will line back up and put on a cast that you must wear for six to seven weeks." The inmate worker just sat a tray down with a needle and this small bottle of something clear in it. the doctor took the needle out of the plastic and picked up that bottle and drained some stuff out and told me " Mr. Jones this is going to hurt so get ready for the pain." right as he said that he stuck that long ass needle in my thumb and i screamed i got water coming out my eyes. They started laughing at me. he pulled the needle out and then squeezed my thumb so that the stuff would spread all over the broken part of the bone. three minutes later he

BEHIND THESE WALLS

Took my thumb and pushed it forward and snapped it backward. he said. "there you go Mr. Jones that was easy now let me put your cast on." in ten minutes I'm walking out the doctor office and back in the van I sat thinking that when the numbness go away the pain will come.

I'm walking to Oak dorm to see Blue. I see these guys by this building everybody is in a circle, i got closer and I see a preacher in all white and this guy in this big metal tub, he's being baptized. i stood there and watched for four guys get baptized. i didn't know that prison do baptizing. I never been baptized before. after they was done I walked over to the pastor. I said. " sir excuse me how can I get baptized?." he looked at me and smiled and said. " son you want Jesus as your Lord and savior?." " yes I do, i want to be saved." I said. with a big and humble smile on his face and said. " our next time we baptize will be next Friday. if you're serious, go inside and sign your name in the book that's on the desk and you come to church next Thursday. That's when we have service, okay." i said. " okay I'll be there, thank you."

I wonder why Mamma never got me baptized when I was a baby. she had us in church every Sunday and everyone in our family went to church.

I see this black dude standing in front of Blue's dorm. I said. " bro could you go get Blue for me?." he said. " Willie Jones?." I

BEHIND THESE WALLS

Said. " Yeah, is he in there?." "hold up let me go check. no he caught the chain this morning." he said.

Blue is gone. We only got to hang out only two days. I wouldn't mind doing my time at this prison this is a kick back spot.

It's eight o'clock and it's dark out side and everyone is going to the gym to watch the movie. I walked inside and it's dark. i see why the homies told me to wait by the door because you could easy get messed up in here. I see the homies and they got a seat saved for me. i never got the name of the movie but when that lady showed her tits everyone started yelling from the sight of one tit. the movie was okay what little I seen. i was more looking over my shoulder more than watching the movie, so i'm cool on this.

I told the homies that I will be getting baptized this Friday. they was happy for me. But they said that they won't be able to come which was cool with me. I got to get this done. I might not make it out of this prison alive so i got to get my soul, spirit in line with the Lord, because i know all prisons is not laid back like this one. this is a start to get myself mentally , physically and spiritually sound for this long ride.

Today is the day I get saved. i'm not nervous or feeling any shame. the sun is out. i walked over to where there are fifteen to twenty guys standing. I got on a white gown and my boxers. i'm walking toward the tub that's filled with water. I can feel the Holy spirit inside me. the people around the tub are singing "Glory Glory Hallelujah" and i'm standing in the tub. I got a plastic bag

BEHIND THESE WALLS

Over my cast. two guys had went before me and now it's my turn. the water is cold and the pastor said. " Albert your now accepting the Lord as your personal savior and to forgive you of all your sins. bless you Albert in the name of the father the sone and the Holy spirit I baptized you." I was then laid in the water and when me head went under. I felt different for five seconds that I was under. i felt like a new man and my spirit was lifted like never before. I stepped out and everyone started clapping i gave them a smile. after everyone got baptized we got be hind the tub with one hand on it thew pastor said. " together tip the tub over. your sins will be forever forgiven, Amen." we went back into the church and there i was given my first ever communion. we sang some songs and service was over.

I walked to the weight pile and the homies are getting their buff on. Sta-Soft said. " ru-al did you get baptized, I got baptized when I was a baby?." I said. " yeah blood." Big Mike is getting his buff on and he got his twenty one inch arms on tight. I notice that he is missing a finger but that is not slowing him down. I'm standing there watching the homies buff iron when I see the crip dude start talking shit to this Mexican guy and it's a very heated argument. everyone stopped lifting weights and all eyes are on them. We walked over there to see what's up. The Mexican guy is talking shit in Spanish and then in English. He said. " This dude came over here and took our weights and didn't ask if he could used them, so i told him to put them back, and he said no."

PRISON LIFE

The crip said with a lot of anger. " Cuzz wasn't using them so i took them." This crip got some size on him too. Big Mike is the biggest on the weight pile and Sta-Soft is the next biggest on the whole yard he got some nineteen inch arms, standing five-eleven and two hundred and fort pounds of all muscles. dark skinned and a big afro. that made him stand out.

Big Mike spoke in Spanish and I don't know what he said but the Mexican guy said. " okay, you can use the weights but when you're done bring them back." the crip said. " okay i'll bring them back, thank you Big Mike." everybody went back to what they was doing.

To watch Big Mike handle that situation he did it with some real class and gangsta in it. it could have got turned into a big ass race riot. but blood kept his cool and didn't raise his voice or mean mug anybody. and everybody is back to their program. I like the way blood handle that. it was real smooth. i just learned something. it don't always have to be violence, things can get talked over settled in peace. This is the weight pile where guys come to release stress and anger and take it all out on them weights but the human body can become that target. When it's time to get down i will know. I was ready but this was not one of them times.

After the homies workout we walked some laps around the track and i noticed a lot of guys saying what's up to Big Mike and Sta-Soft and they gave that nod of respect back to them. I like that. this is so different from the blood module and and L.A. county jail. it's not

PRISON LIFE

All about riding on crips. but i'm not going to let my guard down on them. I notice that the bigger you are the more respect you're going to get. I like the way that they carry their prison status. you don't have to throw your weight around and being a bully. when I get my size I'm not going to a bully.

I left to dorm early so i wouldn't be late for classification. i got my ducat last night for nine o'clock. the building wasn't hard to find. there are two benches in the front. i took a seat and they started calling off names and mines was in the first three names being called. i walked in and this inmate worker sitting behind a desk said. " Mr. Jones go to room two, the counselor is waiting for you." I took a deep breath and walked in and this short bald headed man is sitting behind his desk. he said. " okay, Mr. Jones this is your classification to determine what type of prison you're going to do your time in. it's about the levels, and there are four levels. I will ask you about twenty five questions and then i will tell you what level you're going to.

He asked some crazy questions but we got it done. he wrote on this piece of paper for three minutes. i'm looking at the wall and then he broke the silence. " Mr. Jones, you have forty six points. that makes you a level three and the border line of a level four. so i put you down for w level three prison." he said. I looked at him not knowing what the hell he was talking about. I said. " what's the difference from a three to a two?." he answered. " you will in a cell and not a dorm like you're living here. your points can go

PRISON LIFE

Down every six months and you could end up on a level two or one after a couple of years. it's up to you on how you do your time. i put you down for tow prisons, Solano and Folsom. both prisons are up north. you will be leaving within ten to fifteen days. as of right now you have a release date of July. 1988 it might seem like a long time but you will se how fast it goes by. so good luck Mr. Jones.' I said. " thank you sir."

I walked to the homies dorm to tell them what happen. the home boy Outlaw had left two days ago and there is only three bloods on the yard. Sta-Soft in up here on a ninety day observation for some kind of murder that happened in San Diego on an undercover pig in a drug raid and Big Mike is only doing four months so they will both be leaving soon also.

I get to their dorm and they are chillen under a tree on the side of the dorm. i told them that i will be leaving soon and i told them the prisons i might be going to and Big Mike said. " so you will be starting your time, that's bool. Solano is one of your choices. that pen is okay. it's new when you go to a new prison everybody is jockying for positions and a lot riots jump off. the good thing is you can get a job fast. as for Folsom it's an old prison. they got very small cells but it's bool up there also. no matter where you go, there will be some other b-dogs. you'll be okay because your a down b-dogs and them O.G.s you talked to in that blood module smart homies. and it's hard to be a blood, HA! HA!,"

PRISON LIFE

I learned alot from these two O.G.s I know that they will be getting out soon and I'll see them on the streets some day.

I woke up to a voice saying. " Mr. Jones, get up your going to catch the chain in ten minutes. don't forget to bring your locker lock." I got out of bed and went to the bathroom and got myself together. I looked at the clock and it's four o'clock I had stayed up late watching T.V. I don't have anything to take with me. i gave all i had left to the black guy in the bunk next to mines. I gave the c/o the lock. I learned in the blood module to leave all food and other things behind for that good karma.

Walking to R&R it's a cold chill in the air the sky is clear. it's going to be another nice sunny day. i get in the holding tank and there are about fifteen other guys already here. I only see two other black guys and they don't bang. the c/o came and said. "okay guys the bus is on the way, so let's get this out the way. put all your state blues into that big plastic bag and put on one of them orange jump suits. once you're done, you will be handcuffed with waist chains and ankle cuffed. You're going to Solano prison and it will take about eight to nine hours to get there."

I got on the waist chains and I don't feel disrespected like i was in the county jail. i can hear the bus pull up and somebody said. " the gray goose is out there." I'm like, why did he call the bus the gray goose?. I walk outside and see that bus is much bigger than the county jail bus and it's gray and green with some prison bars

PRISON LIFE

Wrapped around the windows. now i see why they call it the gray goose. i stepped on and it has plush big seats and it's warm. everyone got on and five minutes later we are going through the big gates and on the freeway. i'm getting my look of real freedom. I better get some sleep.

I slept for four hours and now i need a smoke but i don't have any. there are three prison guards on the bus, two in the front and one in a cage in the back by the rest room and he gat a mini fourteen rifle and a big ass hand gun. The c/o said. " Guys we're going to stop at burger king for lunch in about two hours." I'm surprised to know that we will be stopping as burger king. i thought that they was going to give us a bag lunch. the bus pulled over to the side of the freeway and one officer got off. fifteen minutes later with tow big bags in his hand. I'm looking out the window as he walked back to the bus. he passed out one Whooper, fries and a tall soda. i got this food on my lap. i ate it and it tasted good. looking out the window i see one house every three miles i know it must feel good to live in the country like this. I see a sign that said. " Solano state prison next exit." it's two o'clock when we pulled up to the prison. i looked at the buildings and they are all gray concrete with a lot of long windows. i can see on the yards guys walking, jogging on the track. the bus drove through the big gates and stopped next to this double wide trailer and on the door it said. "R&R". we got off the bus and got the cuffs off and we're

BEHIND THESE WALLS

placed in three small holding tanks. the officer said. " i will be back." And shut the door we can't see anything.

Two inmates came in with the c/o and one took our clothe size and shoe size. the other worker got bed rolls and passed them out with a fish kit. i looked in my fish kit and there was a box of Deukmejian tobacco. i hurries up and rolled me one. within two minutes all three tanks are full of smoke. the inmate came with our clothes and shoes and mine fit just right. after about thirty minutes the c/o came and said. "it's time to go, so when i call your name give me your C.D.C. number and i'll tell you what yard and building you're going to and once you get there the building officer will tell you what cell you're in. i will make two lines and the officer will escort you to your yard and building.

I'm on yard two building eight. walking through three gates to the yard, i'm looking around I'm like a tourist in amazement that i'm about to spend three years of my life behind these walls. I got to make the best of it. my heart is beating fast and i walk by the weight pile. guys are looking at me and the other dudes. once i seen all the red my heart slowed back down to it's normal beat. i see Mexicans and brothas with their red flags on their heads and some got them around their wrist. while looking at them i hear a voice " ru-al! ru-al! over here, blood." i look and it's pudden, i'm happy to see a face that i know. i said. " what's up big homie, it's been a while, i see we're back together again."

he said. "Yes we are, when you get yourself together come to the weight pile I'll be here waiting on you." I couldn't stop because I was being escorted by the c/o so i gave him a nod. It feels good to know that blood is here. Damn, blood got real big since i last seen him. i get inside and i look around and it's big in here and they have a big T.V. and some benches where you can sit and watch it. the officer walked into the office and came out with this other c/o and he said. " I'm the building officer. my name is officer green. When i call your name i'll give you your cell. Jones you're in cell sixty eight. once you get everything together come back to the office so i can tell you about your program."

I walked into the cell and it's much bigger than the cell in Chino. i made up my bed and I looked at the photos on the wall and i see this big ass dude with a red flag on his head. he got to have some twenty inch arms and he's on the yard with other bloods. the cell has a good smell to it and it's very clean. everything is put in the right place. the music is still playing on his boom box. he got a T.V. on the shelf. i rolled up a few smokes and went to c/o green office. he told me about the program which is cool and then i walked outside.

I got to the weight pile and Pudden walked up with this older person and said. " ru-al you remember the homie Yap, who was in 3600 blood module with us?." I said. " Yeah, i remember you, blood, you had that fight with 187. What's up blood?." Pudden asked me how much time i had and I told him five years. he then introduced me to a lot of b-dogs. it got to be at least fifteen on the weight pile and they all got some size on them. This blood walked up and said. " I'm gangsta Sam from L.P.P. what cell are you in?." I told him, " yeah your in the homie Big Dan's cell, blood is bool, he's from Inglewood Family Gang." G-Sam said.

So far i've met about twenty bloods, some Northern brothers and Northern Mexicans they all got some yokes. C.J., Bountry AL both from the MOB are working out together and they got some size on them and her I am with a cast on my hand and i want to workout so bad. I got to be the smallest blood here. Yap walked up and said. " ru-al when you get that cast off you can workout with me and Pudden." I said. " I got five more week with it on. i can't wait to get it of. I broke it fight Smooth in the blood module and i hit him wrong." Pudden said. " I'm in Building nine you're in blood head quarters so you will be okay. I'll get you a nice care package and i know the other homies is going to do the same so when they do accept it because it's blood love with no strings attached. It's almost dinner time and when it's over I'll put you up on the program and the yard okay?." I said. "okay"

It's count time and Big Dan just got back from wrok. he walked up the stairs and the gun man that's in the inside tower he got a hand gun on his hip and a mini 14 rifle on a strap on his shoulder. he got control on who come in or out their cells. he let Big Dan in. I'm already standing i was looking out the door window.

BEHIND THESE WALLS

I said. " What's up blood I'm ru-al from A.P.B. I;m your new cellie." We shook hands and did it with a "B" and he said. " I'm Big Dan from I.F.G. what's up ru-al?. Blood you're welcome to anything in this cell and no you don't have to ask, all i ask you to do is that you keep the cell clean which we clean every week. So from this day until next week I'll clean and you will clean for a week. other than that we are bool." I said. " okay blood i got you." blood is much bigger close up. I didn't meet all the bloods in this building yet but i know that it's more. Big Dan told me about this building and the crips on this yard and who we get alone with and don't. Count is over the Big Dan is flashing the cell light and the c/o in the tower open the cell door. I was told every hour they have an un-lock the guard will let you in the building or in your cell at that time. We went downstairs and i see the home boy from Miller Gangsta, Joint i have not seen blood in years and we hugged he told me that he got some extra state boots so i don't have to wear these thin and flat shoes the prison gave to me. We all walked to the chow hall together and it's about twenty five bloods damn this is a lot of bloods. we ate and went to the weight pile. The homies that worked doing the day can't work out so they workout after dinner. I'm waiting for Pudden to get through eating with his building. I'm looking at the homies get their buff on and Big Dan he got eight 25 pound plates on the bench bar and he got them making alot of noise with each rep all eyes are on him and what he is doing with them eight quarters.

BEHIND THESE WALLS

Pudden came to the weight pile and he had to show me that he can lift them eight quarters which is four hundred pounds. As we are walking he is talking and I'm all ears. he letting me know everything there is to know about this prison and the people in it. the first thing he said." ru-al we are not tripping on the crabs. we show them they respect and they show us ours. we do have our allies. you seen all those brown brothers (MEXICANS) and the other brothas on the weight pile?. they are from up north. The mexicans from up this way don't get alone with the Mexicans from down south. you will see them wearing their blue rags. as time pass you will meet them all so you will know who to help if they need it. because they have our backs and we got there and you never want someone to say " where you was when the smoke cleared." because if something big jump off you want to be there what that smoke clear."

We get to the other side of the prison yard and when I seen a sea of blue rags everywhere it was a different world the crips are working out and the Mexicans are too. it had to be at least fifty crips and the same with Mexicans and their are a lot of white guys too. Pudden said. " ru-al this is where they hang out and do their time. you can see the Mexicans I told you about and the white guys as well hang out back here. the crips has two main buildings, eleven and twelve. no bloods live on this side this is their spot.

They had blue rags on everyone and all the weights they are criping hard back here. I see so big ass crips too and Mexicans.

BEHIND THESE WALLS

Some of the crips are saying hi to Pudden and he saying it back to them and some of the Mexicans. I see how big these dude are i got to get this cast off so i can catch up. bloods are on side of the yard and the crips on the other side. I see that is keeping the peace.

I said. " we get alone with the northern Mexicans and the northern brothers but you said something about B.G.F.s who are they?."
"B.G.F. stand for Black Gorilla Family, They are one of the oldest black prison gangs. Any kind of race riot they will be there." Pudden said.

We walked the track about four times and he was doing all the talking and I'm listing to every word. The sun went down and we are still outside they have big lights that lit up the whole yard.

Four weeks has passed and I asked Yap to take off my cast. He said. " let's go to the sink. we got to get it wet and it will be easy to come off." he wet it and it got soft and he slid it off and that felt so so good. I started rubbing my skinny hand and that was feeling good. he said. " wait for two weeks before you start lifting weights because you don't won't to break it again." I said. " thank you O.G."

My first day working out it's me, Pudden and Yap. Pudden is showing me the best way to lift weights. i got the jacket on that G-Sam gave me. he told me to always wear it then you can hide your muscles and no-one can size you up. so i got on this jacket in this sun and at the heat of the day. Pudden said. " ru-al the best way to get motivated is to pick out someone that's buffing iron every

BEHIND THESE WALLS

Day and you put in your mind that you're going to catch him but make sure it's someone that is just a little bigger that you. you will see your progress and then you find someone else and you pass him up. " "Okay big homie." I said.

I got my first full week of working out and my body is sore. Bountry AL gave me my first red flag I'm wearing it on my head. The homie Joint gave me some workout gloves. Big Dan bought me some brand new tennis shoes. they are showing me some real blood love. today I got my muscles measured and i got some fourteen inch arms and i weight one hundred and thirty pounds. I got a lot of work to do and just enough time to make it happen but for know I'm the smallest b-dog.

We got one home boy from Lincoln Park Blood out of San Diego i never seen a blood as cool as he is. this blood got a walk that no-one else has and he got a small sag in his pants and he is on swole it some eighteen inch arms and a long ass perm in his hair. He got a real gangsta walk and style about his self and he wear his green flag on his head. he is the one i"m going to catch i know i got to work out twice a day and that is what I'm going to do.

Today I'm going to the gym to play some basketball and work on my legs. i don't want to be one of them guys that got big arms and skinny legs. and in here they have all the leg work out machines. I see this where we on this yard get to talk to the homies on yard

BEHIND THESE WALLS

One. I walked over there to meet the homies and the first person I see is the homie from my hood G-Mutt he is in for a murder he didn't do. he has been down two years already. we talked for a while. I also met Reno from Family Swan hood. blood has one of the longest jheri curls I ever did see on a person head. they don't have that many bloods on their yard. I talked to G-Mutt every chance i got. he wanted me to move to his yard but i was bool on this yard.

I got a job. I'm a dorm porter. it's like being a trust-b i get twenty four dollars a month and that was cool because i didn't get any money from home, Wayne sent me my first care package from home so big bro did that for me. I wanted to get a job in the kitchen but they was not finished on building it. We ate all our meals in building nine and the crips ate their meals in building ten. Also in building nine is where they have the canteen. this is a very new prison and there are a lot of empty cells in every building. So with this porter job I'm last to get locked up and i get to roam.

Me and Golddie from V.N.G. had become real close and when the homie Speedy from D.L.G. came Big Dan moved into his cell and i moved into Golddie's cell. every Friday night we would watch W.W.F. wrestling and then we would put each other in a move to see if we could get out of it. he's much bigger than me. i could never get out of his hold but it made me stronger each time we did it.

PRISON LIFE

I've been here a year now and there has not been any dram for my first year here I just knew that there would be some. I got into more shit in the blood module. i have been working two times a day, in the morning with Pudden and Yap and after dinner with Joint and Frog from N.H.B. Frog likes to bench press and do top ness. he can hit six quarters three hundred pounds and me I'm hitting just three quarters. Big Dan is now hitting ten quarters five hundred pounds. he was repping it ten times a set with ease. damn blood is strong. the homie G-Sam has started braiding my hair and it has got long. today he's going to teach me how to braid my own hair. it's didn't take long for me to learn.

The homie Sugar Hill from Lincoln Park went home and I did catch him on my sizes and I picked out this other guy. Me, Joint and Frog is getting our buff on. when this crab came out of building seven name Kelso he is almost bigger than Big Dan. He walked by our weight pile, Joint said. " Blood why are you red eyeing me?." Kelso said. " Cuzz i'm not dead eyeing you." Joint walked up on him, which Joint was two feet taller but the crab was bigger. I'm looking at this and knowing this is going to be that time for a fight. Out of no where Joint socked Kelso in the eye and then put up his fist to fight. when that happen me and Frog walked over there. i looked at this big crab and he's holding his eye and he didn't swing back. he walked away and didn't say anything to Joint. Joint said. " get your bitch ass away from our weight pile blood with your big scary ass."

PRISON LIFE

I just seen a homie punk the biggest crab on the yard. he didn't even swing back if he would had he would have got his ass kicked but damn nothing he is a buster. Everyone stopped working out because he walked toward his weight pile and that is where all his home boys are. I'm going to be in my first big prison riot. The S.A.s and other brothers are waiting on them to come around the track. ten minutes pass and nothing so we started back working out but we are ready just in case they do come.

I'm thinking WOW blood just punked that crab he stole on him and he walked off with his tail between his legs. I know that Joint can fight but just did one punch and it was over. to see blood in action he kept it gangsta. there was no need to keep talking it was heated enough to fight and BAM! one to the eye and it's over. later on that night the other crips had found out what happen and they beat kelso up and rolled him up off the yard. and once again he didn't even fight back. he was all mouth and muscles and turned out to be a cream puff.

I'm here two years now and Golddie went home. he left me his T.V. and i moved into the cell with C.J.. We was talking one night and I said. " blood you look like someone i was in 3600 blood module with. do you know a homie named Black Bird?." " Yeah I know him, That's my big brother." he answer. I said. " blood i have been wanting to ask you that for a year now.." me and C.J. became bool cellies we stayed up late night telling was stories, he's another big ass blood six foot three and some twenty inch arms. he had some good war stories.

PRISON LIFE

I got some size now I measure myself after two years and i some seventeen and a half inch arms and my chest is out there too. But I still got a long ways to go because I want to get bigger. Still no encounter with any crips. it is different here but i still got some time to do.

The Homie Hit Man from the Jungles went home yesterday. we have been cooking some big spreads for the homies that was going home. We want to send them out to the streets with a lot of prison brotha love. I know Hit Man is enjoying his daughter, he would take her photo everywhere even on the weight pile. She looks just like blood.

I go to the library once a week to read the L.A. Times news paper and check up on all the high profile cases. The last time i came in here I seen that they sent Pee-Wee to death row blood had a homie already there Big Time both from Family Swan. and now I'm reading about Ase Kapone being found guilty and he was sent to death row and we thought the he was going to beat his case. I hope them bloods on death row stay safe and strong. That is a different level of doing time.

This year I'm on the flag football team. each building has a team, we haven't lost a game all season. Building twelve only lost one game and that was to us. so it's the crabs headquarters against the bloods headquarters. this is our super bowl. we got the red flags and they got the yellow flags. I'm playing middle line backer. the homie from San Fransico is our quarter back. he played some college

PRISON LIFE

Ball and he got an arm. we got some (P.L.R.) Professional Low Riders out of Palo Alto and some brothas from Oakland. the one guy from Richmond named Memphis, everybody thought he was soft because he got a long perm when curled it went to the middle of his back and he got some size on him this is his first year playing on the team. he have been hitting them crips hard and he had called out two crips to fight but they ate some cheese.

It's a warm summer day and the game started. the crips scored twice on two long bombs. the time went by so fast. it's already the third quarter and it's twenty one to seven. they have been beating us on big plays. and they are talking big shit. they got the ball and about to score again and if they do this game is over. I can hear them crabs on the sideline saying. " we got this game Cuzz, let's show them how we get down." We are not saying anything because we are getting beat. the guards are standing on the sideline so the game don't get out of hand because they know that it's the Crips and bloods playing. " we need a stop bad." Big Dan said. the crip went back to pass and he threw the ball on my side i snatched the ball out the air and took off running toward our end zone. I'm running as if the police is chasing me. I scored the touchdown and the homies went brazy. i was so happy i did a round off flip flop, flip flop back. and the homies was like " damn ru-al we didn't know you know you could tumble like that." I never told anyone that i can tumble i just never flipped and i had to after that. but that was short lived we're still behind by seven points. we tied the

PRISON LIFE

Game up at twenty-one apiece. the crips got the and the first team to score will win the game.

In our defensive huddle, C.J. said. " blood, we got to get that damn ball back and beat these crabs. we come too far to lose this game, so somebody got to make a play on the ball." We put our hands together and said. " Dorm Eight." we got the biggest homies on the front line. somehow we got to put a stop to this drive and they are marching down the field. I have been sticking this crip Ice Man. he's my size and he has been talking shit through out the whole game. we have been hitting each other hard. he's a wide receiver he had already caught a touch down on me. C.J. Said. "ru-al if they throw that ball to him, stop him even if you got to hit" just as we knew, they threw the ball to him i jumped in front of him and took the ball and started running toward our goal line. I got a death grip on the ball running down the side line. I can hear the homies saying. " run ru-al, run blood," and i can hear the crips saying. " stop him Cuzz! stop him!." out of no where i got tackle from behind. and it was Ice Man, i jumped up and said. " blood why the fuck did you tackle me? this is flag football." he looked at me with anger in his eyes and said. " Cuzz that's the only way I could have stopped you ru-al." The crowed broke up and i know that i would have done the same . we got the ball close to the goal line. The homies are happy we got what we needed. know we got to win so we can go eat some ice cream. after all the hugs we still got a game to win. the crabs are mad. we got into our huddle, i'm glad that they let me stay on the offense. I'm a decoy wide receiver, C.J. said. " okay Big Dan we are going to run the ball behind you on a quarter back sneak." C.J. got under the center. out of nowhere someone said. "bring it on." hike! C.J. got the ball and the held it for two seconds and Big Dan mowed down two crabs and then C.J. ran right behind him and ran in the end zone and we won the game. we was happy to win this game. we went 12-0. no team had ever done that. the crips held their heads down but we showed them some respect and good sportsmanship and shook their hands, i never touched so many crips in my life, unless i was putting my fist on them. We went to the store and everybody got ice cream and sodas and I got extras because i was the reason we won and that felt good. Ice Man said, " good game ru-al." i know that he hated that lost and I said. " good game Ice man."

Hanging out by the canteen and Big Dan still had about twenty dollars of funny money (PRISON MONEY) he spent it all on junk food for us to eat. we're talking about the game and I told them about the hood football game i had against "THE WEAK SIDE". me and G-man was the star in that game. It's a lot of people hanging out by the canteen buying food and this is where the Homosexuals hang out to sell booty. they are here every Saturday's. Some Mexicans guys are selling their art work. this spot is like a hood swap meet.

After two years of being a door porter i got a new and higher paying job in (P.I.A.) Prison Industry Authority. I'm working with six other guys in our are we are making prison bunks and i'm getting thirty six dollars a month and the pay goes up every three months or if i'm doing a good job i can get a faster raise. I could get up to an A-3 pay number and that's one hundred and fifty six dollars a month. I won't be here that long to get that kind of money. I should have got this job when i first got here. I'm learning how to wield. this will help me when i get out and get a job. i only have one friend in this whole prison. he's a Mexican older guy. he don't gang bang and he's from L.A. and the homies seem to like him too. Romero Calderon which I call him Rel-Roo, we became real good friends he's in for murder he got ten years for killing this guy that tried to break into his place again. Rel-Roo said. " he was sitting in his living room and it was dark knew that these two guys would come back when I'm gone. I parked my car around the corner and came in the back. I'm waiting one came through the window and as soon as he got half way in I shot him in the chest with my shot gun. I was eating some nachos and cheese and I sat the gun down and called the police and know here I am. Man they broke into my house one time to many." he gets family visits and when he go for his three days and come back he would bring back some weed for me. He didn't smoke but he knew that i did and he would bring back some good weed and give all to me and I'll share with the homies that smoked weed.

PRISON LIFE

Working for six months now in P.I.A. and i got a few pay raises. I' getting seventy three dollars a month it's a B-3 pay number. I'm saving all my money because i'm on my way out of this prison. I liked eating my lunch with Rel-Roo in his work area and for the past four days this tall skinny white dude been messing with this short Mexican guy. They are arguing again and this time it's much more intense than any other time. The Mexican guy walked off and the white guy got his chest stuck out as if he just punked that guy. Fifteen minutes later the Mexican guy came back. he got this big ass shank in his hand and i know where he made it at. right next to my work area. they do the cutting of metal for shelf's and lockers. I got a good look at the shank and it got these deep cuts on both sides and it's about nine inches long and thick. I heard about them kind of shanks they are called Christmas trees and his do look just like one. that kind of shank goes in and when it's pulled out the body flesh comes out because of the the cuts on it and it go in easy but coming out is where it do it's damage. Me and Rel-Roo is looking at what is about to go down, I'm not about to say shit it's not my beef. the white guy got his back turned while eating his lunch. the Mexican guy said. " say bitch i told you to stop fucking with me, i'm no punk." the first stab went into his side and when he pulled the shank out it was bloody and flesh came out with it. the white dude made a loud scream and i can't believe what i'm seeing. The little Mexican guy started talking in Spanish

PRISON LIFE

To the white guy. he hit him about three more times and that shank got meat hanging off it and blood dripping. he's talking shit and stabling the shit out of this whit dude. he's trying to kill him. it's blood every where in that area. the Mexican is standing over him talking in Spanish. the superviser which is a free person non-c/o seen what was going on, he hit the buzzard on the side of his hip and about ten c/o's came running telling everybody to step back. I didn't move from where i was standing. I was kind of in shock. I never seen anybody get stabbed before and this Mexican dude put on a show. He dropped the knife and turned around to get handcuffed. the white guy looked to be dead he is not moving any more. the guards are pumping on his chest and two other officers got his shirt off trying to plug up the many holes so the bleeding can stop. if this dude don't die GOD is on his side because he got at lease seven to eight time and each time flesh came out and now the screaming has stopped and i know i only hear the sirens from the ambulance. they came real fast and they took him. on the ground was a bloody mess. we was told to leave because it's a crime scene.

Walking back to our yard I said. "Rel-Roo, what was he saying in Spanish?." Rel-Roo said." he was tell him that he wasn't no punk and i told your white ass that i will kill you, you stupid son of a bitch." and he did just that. the guards looked down all the yards and did interviews for the next two days. The guards want to see if there going to be any problems between to whites and the Mexicans.

PRISON LIFE

We got off lock-down and we found out that the white didn't die they saved his ass. I just knew that he wasn't going to make as holes he had. that was my first time seeing something like. that white guy is one lucky dude. now i see what the O.G. homie Big Mouse was saying, " your mouth can be your worst enemy." and i just seen that first-hand and being a bully that's what he get.

Alot of the old homies went home and a new batch has come. Mookie from D.L.G., Lonely Man from the Pueblos and Little Bo Slim from W.S.P. I was surprise to see him, we was in high school and job corps together now in prison our lives are coming full circle.

I got some yokes know me and Frog has been buffing iron twice a day for almost two years. I got some eighteen and a big chest and tree trunks for legs. I walked in the building and this big ass crab bumped into me I said, " watch where you're going blood." he spoke in a deep voice and said. " fuck you, you slob. you better watch where you're going cuzz." This crab got me by hundred pound and as big as a house. but i know that don't mean anything on how big you are. from what i seen the homie Joint did to kelso and he didn't fight back and I know that I'm no punk and everyone in this area heard all that was said. I know that I"m no buster so I said. " fuck it lets go t my cell and get them up." " let's go cuzz, i'm going to mop your ass up." he said. on our way to my cell, Big Dan said. " hold up you big ass bitch! you think I'm going to let you fight my little homie? you're full of shit, blood." I said. " I got this blood, fuck that crab." it's my time to get my strips. I see

BEHIND THESE WALLS

That look in Big Dan's eyes. he he want this crab because he had been walking around in this building like he's super hard and this is our headquarters. And true enough Big Dan Said. " back up ru-al i got this. he been walking around like he's hard. I'm going to pull his whole card and see what he got, you can get the next one blood."

They walked up the stairs and we sat at the table and some of his homies sat at the other table. David, the carb walked in first and Big Dan walked in right after him. they didn't close the door because if they did they'd be in there for a whole hour and i know the homie will put him under the bunk. we can look inside cell from where we was sitting. I see the homie scoked him two time. he hit the crab so fast and hard, somehow they got turned around and now the crab got his back to the door. Big Dan pushed him with both hands to get him off him and the crab came flying out the cell and he almost flipped over the railing and his ass would have fell over to the ground. he caught him self from that fall that would have put him in the hospital. he didn't get a punch in, he grabbed his eye that was swelling up and walked down the stairs and he didn't say shit to us or his home boys they got up and followed him to his cell. this is the second time i seen the homies sock a crab and they didn't do shit. Big Dan came down and said. " ru-al i know you wanted him but have waiting for this moment for months as you can see he's a buster. I know that you would have got him but I didn't want to chance it and let that crab get a strip on a B-dog and

BEHIND THESE WALLS

That's what he was trying to do. I know you're down and ready blood I had to get him." I said. " okay blood i got the next one. i like the way you put hands on him."

I got eight month left. i went to the doctor yesterday to see if i could get circumcised. the doctor set it up a date for me to get it done. two weeks later i got the ducat to go to Vacaville prison which is only ten minutes away. they have the hospital for the operation. just me and one c/o drove in the van to the prison. once inside it's like a whole different world. I'm looking at some pretty looking women walking these halls. it's girls standing around talking and I'm walking with my chest sticking out as we pass them, the guard said. " you see them men over there." he had pointed two that group of women. I said. " no i didn't see any men, just them women we just passed." "Jones you just seen some Homosexuals, this is their prison. all of them are men. they all got homo shots to stop their face hair from growing and they get shots to make their tits grow and the prison gives them the shots. all them are guys you just seen. i see that they had you fooled." he said. they sure had me fooled because they looked just like a women. they got long silky hair perms and big tits and the way they have their pants are tight. I got to watch what i lust on because it could be a man. They didn't look like the Homosexuals in Chino prison these are looking like real women.

We get to the operation room, i put on the gown that was given to

BEHIND THESE WALLS

Me, and my ass is hanging out. i got on the operation table on my back and the nurse is putting the needle in my arm for the I.V. she then put this shield in front of my face where i can't see what they going on. " Okay Mr. Jones, count to hundred." The nurse said." I remember counting to eleven and i was out i woke up from the anesthesia, i see the guard sitting in a chair next to me. I said. " how long was I out?." the c/o answer." about twenty minutes, they cut off your foreskin and that shit looked crazy and painful man you got heart to get this done at your age." Sitting in this waiting room the doctor came in and said. "how do you feel Mr. Jones? you will feel a little woozy, that will wear off in about ten to fifteen minutes. now Mr. Jones you got stitches on your penis which should fall off in two weeks also, no nude magazines because if you get an erection you will bust the stitches and you'll have to get it done over and the pain will be unbearable so you got to be careful. so enjoy your new penis when you get out." The c/o helped me up after fifteen minutes I can walk. walking down the hallway i got this cowboy walk because i don't want to rub it up against my pants. I'm in the van on my way back, it seemed like the c/o drove over every bump in the road, i'm glad that I'm still numb. i get back to the yard and a few homies was waiting for me to get back. they know that i was going to get this done I'm walking with my legs wide open and one homie made a slap motion like he was going to hit me in my dick. i put my hand in front of it and said. "blood stop playing, i got to get to my cell before the numbness go

BEHIND THESE WALLS

Away." I get to the cell and the homie Bear from B.H. had moved his stuff to the upper bunk. this was his month to have the bottom bunk but since I'm like this he let me get it. I had to take off two weeks of work I got enough earned time off. I'll still get my day for day time. after a few days I came down stairs. I have not called home since been here or have I sent home any photos of me. But i want to talk to Mamma about why i didn't get this done when I was a baby.

" Hi Mamma how are you doing? it's been a long time since i last talked to you.' I said. Mamma said " hey son, yes it's been a long time i know you should be almost ready to come home. so what's up?. " i got circumcised three days ago Mamma why didn't i get this done when I was born?." I asked. Mamma said in her loud voice. " None of Y'all boys got it done. I only had to get Paul done because he was sick when he was born. the doctor told me that no boys born in the fifties and sixties they just didn't do it so that's why i didn't get you done." I said. " I got baptized also why didn't i get that done when I was little? you sent us to church every sunday." " Boy, i left that up to Y'all but I'm happy that you got it done. well anything else you got done to your body that you want me to know about?. if so tell me you get home now get off the phone. I love you son and you be careful in there." Mamma said. I said. " okay Mamma I'll see you soon."

I got ten days left. i did three years. i got all my jheri curl products for Yap he's going to hook me up in six days. all the

PRISON LIFE

homie has been telling me to stay inside since i only have ten days left. they don't want me to fuck off my going home date. I never seen any home boys stay in on their last ten days and I'm not going to start. I respect them for that but i got to be down until i leave the yard. Today i hit seven quarters three hundred and fifty pounds and it felt good. For two and a half years of lifting weights twice a day I got to where i wanted to be. I'm on swole. I got nineteen inch arms and a chest that stands out. and nobody on the streets know what i look like.

I'm down to five days left and the homie Goo-Goo from B.H. came he was in another pen. he got life in prison. I had heard about blood. someone told me that he chased two crabs across the yard with tow big ass shanks. he got this crazy ass brother on the streets Gay-Gay. Blood is also a C/k rider in his hood and they both are about five foot six. I can tell he been down because he got some size on him too. I knew that i would be leaving soon so i gave him my red and black Pendleton shirt and my red flag. I like blood.

The northern brothas has been getting into it with the c/o's for the past two weeks one after another they been beating up a c/o going head up with them. That is why when they took off on a c/o it was head up and no lock down for us. I got two days left and standing in line in the chow hall line for dinner. I walked in and the next thing I knew the door got slammed shut and i can hear some bumping on the door and wall. The buzzer went off and the guard inside the kitchen gun tower said. " everybody get on the fucking ground." he got his mini fourteen rifle pointed at u I'm laying on the floor. all the home boys made it inside but there was five 415 brothas behind me. after about ten minutes the guard told us to get up and c/o came in and we asked what happened he said." this black guy that was in line had a fight with one of our officers." Damn if i didn't come in I would have been out there with them and who knows what could have happen. two days to the house and my date could have got fucked up. This is way they say stay in the build and not go outside.

This is my last night before i go home. the homies cooked a big ass spread for me. i like these spreads because that keep our brother hood bond tight and will last forever in here or on the streets. I know if i see any of these bloods on the streets or in another pen we will have that bond. I'm a member of this prison family now.

I got up a little early i got in a good night sleep because it's going to be a long day. I cleaned my self up got my Jheri curl looking good and it's long. I'm going out very new i'm going out with a new un-used circumcised dick I got two tear drops under my left eye one open for my baby that Lisa lost and one closed for doing prison time i got them tattooed after being here one month. I got some nineteen inch arms a big chest and think legs I'm going out these gate as new as anyone doing time can get after three and a half years of the streets and no one has seen the new RU-AL.

PRISON LIFE

I'm getting the full escort to the gate but before I left I had to hit the seven quarters again. about twenty five homies Rel-Roo and all our allies walked me to the gates and before I walked through someone said. " ru-al don't look back." As i'm walking through the gate I did look back I was told if you look back you will come back to prison. i laughed and said. " I love y'all bloods I'm about to TOUCH DOWN.

1989, I'm back on the gray goose with sixteen months I'll do half of that but my violation will eat that up and I'll do a whole year. I'm on my way to Tehachapi state prison I was hoping to go back to Chino. Tehachapi is known as a reception center. after the hour ride from the county jail, the bus pulled up to R&R. this time we got uncuffed inside the building. the building is made like Solano prison. once we got in guys are looking out their cells door windows. me and about twenty five other guys caught the chain we was put into this chain like fence that is connected to two cells so we can used the restroom. At this desk to the side there are three officers and I can see the gun man looking down on us with rifle in hand.

The process begins, one of the c/o's got up and said "okay let's get this over with. it's nine o'clock and it's twenty five of Y'all I want to have everybody in their cells by dinner time so it's up to you on how we get there. The C/O at the desk will call your name and you will tell him what you want to do with your property. if you send it home you got to pay for it. if you got your old C.D.C. number you will keep it if not you will get a new one. you will get

PRISON LIFE

A new one. you will get your photo taken over there where you see my inmate worker. Before you do that I want you to give that worker you clothe and shoe size. When your done you will be give a fish kit. now if anyone wants to act a fool, you see those cages over there? I'll put you in on and you will not like it. do I make my self clear?." "Yes sir." everyone answer.

Everything went real fast. they didn't do half the things that Chino did. I got my old .C.D.C. number because I never got off parole. I got my bed roll and fish kit and that box of Deukemjian tobacco. we ate our bag lunch, then we sat there for three hours. I hear guys yelling out their cells, to guys that they know. The c/o came and gave us or cells, I'm in cell 22. i walked to the cell, looked inside saw this dude, he looked at and gave me a nod. the gun man buzzed my door open and i walked inside and i closed the door behind me. i stuck out my hand and said. " what's up bro? i'm ru-al." he shook my hand and said. "I'm jess." I'm not going to trip if he's a crip. i know he bet not say the wrong thing or it's going to get real ugly up in here. he is a small man so i know that he don't want to test me. I made up my bed in silence. after i was done i rolled up a smoke and sat on the writing desk that is at the back of the cell with a window. I said. " where are you from on them streets?. I'm a blood from Compton." he said, " I don't bang but I'm from Lancaster. I do have some family members that's bloods. they are from Pacoima Piru Bloods (P.P.B.) one you might know his name is B-Barzy. he been in the blood module. I looked at

BEHIND THESE WALLS

Him and smiled because I had just left B-Brazy in the blood module. I said, " yeah i know him. he made it possible for their hood to come in the blood module. He had just about everyday to prove that he and his hood belongs in there and showed that that (P.P.B.s) is a down b-dog hood."

Jess said " we will be eating dinner in about thirty minutes. we eat all our meals inside this building. they will let the bottom tier out first and then the top. The door popped open for chow and I follow Jess. While standing in line i hear someone call my name "ru-al! ru-al up here cell forty-six." I looked up and i can see the face looking down at me but i can hardly see him through that window. i picked up my tray and looked up again once I sat down. oh! hell Naw! I know who that is, it's Smooth. i didn't say anything. i don't want to get put into one of them cages they have. they had put two Mexicans in two of them with their shoes and clothes outside the cage. they just got their boxers on. I'll get at Smooth on the way back to my cell.

This was a good meal for prison food. on my way back i looked up at smooth i see his face very clear know. I said "What's up blood?." and i gave up the "B" with my fingers. Smooth looked at me and smiled and gave up a big ass "C" i seen that, my eyes got big and I shook my head "NO" and he shook his "YES". I couldn't believe what i just seen. i walked into me cell and lit a smoke. NAW!, i didn't see him give up a "C". standing at the door looking out the door window. I didn't say anything to Jess and then they let the top tier out and i see Smooth walking with this dude, that must be

BEHIND THESE WALLS

His cillie. I'm looking at Smooth and he is not that big like he used to be. he's line talking to that dude. I'm going to yell out there, he might get put into one of them small cages.

I said. " Jess you see that dark skinned guy? he was in the blood module with me about five years ago. I lost two fights against him and he gave me two black eyes and a broke nose. I think he's a crab know." jess said. " are you sure that's him ru-al." Man i know who beat my ass I'll never forget that face. damn it's hard to think that smooth is a crip. I do know that crips do accept ex-bloods in their gangs but blood don't do that. he's sucked up to he don't have his size he once had. if he's a crab i'll love to get my hands on him because I'll give him the kick treatment because he turned to crips. I'm on swole, i'll beat his ass." I said.

After dinner they left out four guys to clean the building and one of them dude is the one he was in the chow line with. he came by my cell sweeping. I said. " Sat bro that guy you was talking to in that chow line, he in cell forty six. do you know him?." " Yeah i know him. that's my cellie that my home boy his name is smooth, why?." he asked. I said" Say man I"m a blood and i had some fights with him in the blood module. When i walked to my cell i gave up a "B" and he gave up a "C". is he a crip?." he is fake sweeping in front of my cell so it look like he's doing his job. He said. " I'm a crip and so is he, he ain't never been a blood." I said. " Say bro didn't you hear him call out my name ru-al from your cell? that's me he was calling he said my name twice. I'm ru-al so you see he do know me. the only place I know him from is the blood module so when you get up there ask him if he knows me." " say rual, thanks if he lied to me i'm going to roll up and beat his ass." he said.

I'm in line for breakfast and i look up stairs and the crip dude looked down at me. he gave a motion with his thumb going across his neck and walked away from the door.

Eating my breakfast i see that them two Mexican guys are still in those cages that got blankets on the outside of their cages. one is sitting down eating and the other one is standing up eating. whatever they did it got them spending a night in there. that c/o wasn't lying , you don't want to go in there. These guys had to sleep in them small cages.

After everyone was done eating the workers was let out and that crip dude came to my cell. he said, " yeah, bro, you was right, he was from Fruit Town Brims, and he did say that he know you real good. i told him that he had to leave my cell and he couldn't claim crip." The crip dude went back to his sweeping. I'm very surprised to see that smooth turned crab, he was a rider, he put in work on them now he's one. I'm puzzled. I know this, if i ever see him or get a chance to be around him I'm going to fuck him up.

I got moved to building three. i was so glad. three days of bird bath was not cool. my first day on the yard i met the homies, Bear from east Side pain and B-Down from B.S.V. we're on the weight pile

BEHIND THESE WALLS

And know i"m the biggest on the yard with twenty inch arms I'm on monster swole. it's about six crabs on the other end of the weight pile. they don't want any problems so we didn't trip on them. they only let out one tier every two hours. after we got or buff on we went to this hill that looks over the whole yard. We are chillen when the crips walked by and one of them started red eyeing us and i didn't like that. he is getting his crab walk on. I said. Blood, the next time they walk by I'm going to check that crab that was red eyeing us." B- Down said. " blood, i'm coming with you because before you came in our building that crab has been acting like he run this pen." Bear Spoke. " Oh!, you know I'm coming i don't like the way he's walking either blood."

They walked our way and we walked up on them and they stopped walking. I said to one that got that hard core crab walk and said. " why every time you walk by us your red eyeing us?" " say man I wasn't looking at y'all, we're just walking the track, we don't want any problems with you or your homies." he said." I said. "okay". They walked on and we went back to our spot to hang out. they came around again and none of them looked up at us.

"ru-al you're brazy blood" Bear said, "yeah, that's how b-bads get down, we bring the noise, you see how skinny scary they looked?."
I woke up to a light in myeyes. the c/o said " Jones D-21152 get up, you're catching the chain in ten minutes." i got myself together and rolled up five smokes and said my good bye to B-Down.

BEHIND THESE WALLS

The door opened and I walked out. I see about seven guys already in their orange jump suits. I put mine on. now i got to wait for an escort to R&R.

One hour later the c/o comes to take us to R&R. when i stepped outside it's cold and the wind is blowing hard. I know that the bus is going to warm. I smoked my Last cigarette. I can hear the gray goose pull up. we was told that we are going to (C.M.C.) California Men's Colony prison. It's a four hour ride I'll be able to get some sleep. the ride went by so fast. we pulled up to the prison and the bus drove right through the yard. I can see the dorms. i also see some other buildings that look like level three yards. i don't know how many points i got but i hope I get to kick it in these dorms, but if i got to go on that level three yard I'll do it in a gangsta way.

We got off the bus and walked inside R&R into this small holding tank. this short c/o walked up and said. " all of you men are going to "B" yard it's a level one yard, you seen those dorms as you drove into this prison that is where you'll be living. You will be placed inside an orientation dorm for fifteen days and then you will get your main dorm. this is some easy time but if you want to fuck up you will get sent to East yard and you will not like them small cells and they get hot. My inmate worker will get your clothe and shoe size and you will be given a fish kit. This process will go fast so let's do it gentle men."

I walked into the doom and went to the middle of it and the c/o was waiting on us. we got the dorm rules, beds and locks for the

PRISON LIFE

Lockers. This old prison look just like Chino prison and I'm cool with that. I'm on the top bunk, I made my bed and put what little i had into the locker and went into the T.V. room. this heavy-set brotha walked up to me and said. " I'm monk from B.H. what's up?." I looked at him and wondered how does he know that I"m a blood. I shook his hand and said. " I'm ru-al from A.P.B. nothing much. how did you know that I'm a blood?." He said. " I can tell by your walk. you know us b-dogs got a real gangsta walk and not all crazy like crips so i know my folks. we got about fifteen other b-dogs up here. you will bee them after dinner which is in thirty minutes. if you need anything my bunk is over there. it's about three crabs in this dorm and about twenty five on the whole yard. So you know that we are always out number." he told me about the homies and the program and this should be fun for me.

Walking with Monk from the kitchen we get to these benches there are are nine guys chillen. some got on red tennis shoes, red shirts i knew then that these are the homies. I said. " What's up bloods i'm ru-al from A.P.B." this tall blood introduces himself first. He said. " i'm Kass from the Jungles." he then gave me a big hug, our hoods are big allies on the streets we go by (A.J.) Athens-Jungles. They musta knew that I was coming because this blood walked up with this bag in his hand. He said. " I'm China Man from (C.M.G.) Crenshaw Mafia Gang. this is from all of us, blood." I said "good looking out bloods."

PRISON LIFE

My first six days went well. I'm in the day room watching T.V. and this crip dude kept standing in from of me. the first two times i didn't trip but he is doing it on purpose. I said " say bro can you sit down so I can see the T.V.?. you keep getting in my way." now i know from the blood module that tripping on the T.V. can start some shit. he said. " Cuzz, i can sit or stand when ever i want to what's your fucking problem?." This crab stood five foot six and he got size on him I'm not going underestimate him, Something I'll never do no matter what size they are because I could hit with a lucky punch and it's light out. No one in here knows how big I am because of the big shirt I'm wearing it's hiding my yokes but is he is about to see them. "check this out blood if you don't sit your bitch ass down I'm going to fuck you up" I said. he spoke in a way that impressed his home boys. " fuck you, cuzz you're the bitch." he said. I looked at Monk and smiled. he said. " be bool ru-al he's not worth it blood you just got here and if you get caught your going to the hole." Monk don't know me this is what i like to do. beat crabs asses fighting them no-one is looking at T.V. nay more all eyes on us, my heart is beating fast I can't stop now, i got to perform. I said. " check this out you crab. let's go to the shower and i"m going to beat your ass." We walked to the shower and passed the c/o office and he is doing his paper work he is not going to hear unless this crab scream. the shower is big enough to have a good fight. we both walked in and I took off my shirt because i don't want him to try and grab it. he see how big I am now he want

PRISON LIFE

to talk. I can see the fear in his eyes. he know what is about to happen.

He opened his mouth to talk and i started swinging. the first punch hit him in the nose and the second one caught him right on the jaw. he's still on his feet and i can see the blood coming out his nose he swung one time and missed and than i got him in the eye. i want him to look like the elephant man when he come out this shower and then his home boys will think twice about talking shit to me. i'm putting together some good one-two punches and then he fell. I started kicking him in the head. he started to scream something I hope didn't happen. I just hope the c/o is deep into his work because he is screaming like a bitch. I said. " get your punk ass up blood. I told you i'm going to fuck you up. you want some more?. get up blood." he stayed laying on the wet floor i turned around to walk out and right before i stepped out i turned a shower head on and he's now all wet. the first person i see is Monk. he got this big ass smile on his face, I'm still in my fighting zone. i can't smile yet because one of his home boys might want some. i walked back into the day room to watch T.V. but hoping that he don't snitch on me because I beat him bad. the crab home boys went to get him and on the way out the shower he bump into the c/o real hard so hard that the c/o called other c/o's and they walked the crip dude out the dorm he just (P.C.) up Protected custody. I don't care he could have stayed as long as he kept his mouth shut. But i know his home boys wouldn't let him say after that ass kicking they seen the lumps I gave him.

PRISON LIFE

Word had got out i beat down a crab and all the home boys wanted to know how bad and I said. " real bad, he got the kick treatment."
I moved to dorm six. most of the homies are in dorm eight. it's only me and the homie Maniac from B.H. in this dorm which is all good. Maniac is six foot three with some nineteen inch arms. we became really close and we are the two biggest b-dogs on the yard. Yesterday the little homie JO-JO from (M.G.B.) Miller Gangsta Bloods came. he got kids by the homie Frado's sister Lucie. I heard about JO-JO on the streets riding on them crabs.

another homie came Pitbull from 59 Brims in San Diego. now i'm the second biggest b-dog. he got twenty one inch arms and is super strong. I'm glad that i was taught by some O.G.s that told me about being a bully when you get your size because so many guys die early or come out on the bad end of a fight or shoot out and i don't want that to happen to me. so i let others make that can and I'll react to them.

I have been here for five months and things has been going well everyone is programing. I'm playing some Dominoes and the other homies is enjoying the hot summer day on the grass. this is our spot where we make our spreads and build our bond as homies. we are the only group that dose this bonding. Enjoying our day when this crip dude just got on this yard and he got that walk and he got some size on him. i notice he had been looking at us in a crazy way with about four of his home boys so today i got to say something.

PRISON LIFE

I said " Kass, if that crab walk by us and red eye us like he has been doing for the past three days, I got to call him out." " ru-al let me get this one blood. you're talking about the with the thick glasses?." Kass said. I looked at blood and thought about what Big Dan did in Solano prison. I said. " yeah I'm talking about him he look like Charile tuna and i want him blood, don't trip Kass his home boys will be there too."

They are on their way and true enough he red eyed us. I jumped up first. Kass was too late. my heart is pumping fast so i know that I'm ready. i know that the homies are behind me. I said. " blood why are you red eyeing us when you're walking by. do you have a problem with any one of us bloods?." he looked at me and smiled and said. " cuzz, i can look wherever i want to. you some kind of problem with it cuzz?" I said " hell, yeah, i got a big problem with that blood. fuck it let's kill all the talking let's go to the weight pile weight room. we can get down (fight) in there head up and no guard can see us." he said "lets go cuzz."

A nice size crowd has formed. I'm hoping for a good fight I know i'm going to win but i'm not going to take him lightly because he could get in that lucky punch and T-Roll my black ass. I got a good pumping of blood going in my heart. i had sized him up already just in case we did get down. so i know what I'm up against and he got some size on him. before we started walking toward the weight room where we check out weights it's enough room for us to fight. Kass Said. " ru-al let me get him, blood." I said " it's to o late blood, i already called him out. i got to get down now." I looked at Kass and smiled, we started walking . i had been buffing iron earlier and i took off my shirt and my muscles are still tight. They never seen my yokes because of the shirt i've been wearing. when it's time to get down i got time to take it off i will because i seen to many dude fight with their shirt on and got it pulled over their heads and they got fucked up. so i learn to take mines off. the crabs are walking in the front of us and i see Charlie Tuna look back at me and his eyes got big. he stopped walking. we got ten yards to the shack. this is a good blind spot to fight this is where all the dumb bells are but it's a lot of moving room. I got to make quick work of him because i don';t want him to grab a dumb bell and hit me with it. but if need some help I'm going to clock him up side the head with one. there is no rules or referee's so anything goes in a prison fight. some people think because this is a level one yard it's soft but you can really get messed up real easy.

We walked up on them and I said. " what's up?. let's get this out the way, blood." he spoke with tremble in his voice. " ru-al it's not worth it, i wasn't looking at you or your home boys in a disrespectful way. if you think so i do apologize. i don;t want to fight you man." I said. " check this out bro i'm not here to ride on you or your home boys, but when your walking by like you got a problem with me or my homies i got to say something, so it's squashed." we walked away and my heart calm down. once again i thought about Big Mike in how he handle a situation you don't

PRISON LIFE

Always have to end in violence even though i was ready to fight. the home boy Stone from the Jungles said. " we should just roll up that whole crip car, blood you see them thick ass glasses?. he wouldn't be able to bee ru-al punches anyway. they are lucky that you gave them a pass." JO-JO said. " blood, i'm not for giving them any more passes."

I'm getting my prison reputation by calling out them crabs, and the ones that is stepping up to fight me are losing. So i do understand what JO-JO and Stone is saying because they are younger than me and they want to get their prison reputation as well. since high school I always wanted the ones that thing that are hard core and with that walk. I'm not looking for trouble but i'm ready for when it do come my way. I know that the homies got my back i'm not out here starting shit. and they are going to ride with me until the wheels fall off.

I got three months left and the blood car is getting deep up here and a few new homies has come on the yard. this is know a b-dog yard a lot of the crips went to yard two and there is no bloods over there. We are hanging out by my dorm it's just a few of us talking about life on the streets when three crabs walked out of dorm three and came right toward us and I see the home boy S.A. from (V.T.P.) Village Town Piru, walking behind them. i hope they are not fucking with blood I'm thinking to myself.

PRISON LIFE

The crips get to us and one of them said. " China Man, you need to talk to your home boy, we're looking at T.V. and your home boy kept saying Bompton and we feel he was disrespecting us with his words." the homie S.A. walked up and China Man said. " I'm not a shot caller for any of my home boys here. whatever problem you have with him he can handle it. I can't control his words and neither can you." S.A. is only five foot five and hundred and forty five pounds with a little size. I know blood from the streets and we went to high school together and he's no punk and he was in the riot in high school and riding on them crabs is his thang no matter how big they are. I'm thinking that they feel they would win and we would roll their car up.

S.A. said. "   we're watching the Soul Train music awards and the homie D.J. Quik came on stage flamed up and gave it up to all the homies from Bompton, so i gave it up back to him. and this dude didn't like it so i kept saying it. ru-al, you know me, blood, i'm not going to eat cheese, so if dude want to get down we can go to the shack or the shower. because I'm not going to stop saying it. so what's up?." I looked at the crip dude and said. " so if you got such a big problem with him and his words you don't have no control over, do you want to get down? if not squash it." he crip dude said. " it's not that serious we can squash it." they walked off.

China Man said. " S.A. I don't trust them crabs you got to get some

PRISON LIFE

Heat. you're in that dorm by yourself and we don't want you to get caught slippin. so when it get dark we'll go get you one."

Me, S.A. and China Man is walking the track. the other homies stayed they know that we are going to get blood some heat. we got some nice heat stashed all around the yard so we can be ready at all time. We get to one spot S.A. took watch and China Man dug it up and it's a nice one. he gave it to him and we started back walking the track. the next few days things has calm down in his dorm so we put the heat back. there was no need for him to just walk around with it when the threat is gone.

I don't have to work because i got a solid year to do so I'm just buffing iron and doing my time. everyone else has to work to get their day for day time. no-one got over three years to do so they will be on the streets soon.

after i got out of prison in 1988 I had met some fine women on the streets and my main women is Judy and the rest It was all about the sex. So Judy, Cassandrs and Joann have been taking good care of me doing this time i'm getting extra food packages and tennis shoes and other types of clothes my girls took good care of me. and I'm going to sex them all up when I touch down and they is waiting on me.

I got one month left this time went by so fast. and it was fun on all levels. me and Maniac have been in the same dorm and making spreads everyday. I met some down b-dogs in this pen and China Man has been doing our Saturday spreads and blood can cook. I know when it's time for me to go blood is going to hook up a big spread for me.

I called home and was told that the homie Cyclone got kidnaped and murdered, i was sad to hear that and the way they killed him. people said that he went out like a true gangsta. he was one of our downest homies out there. he will be missed. we have our history he won a fight and i won one but growing up with him and his other brothers "THE BELL BOYS". i know that blood was hated by a few but loved by many and who ever done that is going to pay in some kind of way. I know that them streets are dangerous and sometimes i do feel rescued being in here because that could have been me " If your out on them streets banging and you're caught slippin out there you could easy get ex'd out the game like so many have.

It's time to go home we had a big spread last night and built a strong bond over that meal. I'm saying my good bye's to the homies. i know that the crabs are happy to see me leave but they are not out of the woods because I was helping keep the homies off their asses. but i know that the homies is going to keep them in check if need be. so they are not getting a break from this blood gangsta shit. " Okay, bloods, y'all b-down. don't trip I'll get that package gift to JO-JO girl. I'm gone bloods." I said. as i walked out these prison gates.

BEHIND THESE WALLS

I'm back in Tehachapi reception center, this time for a pistol. Just the last time my violation will eat up the sixteen months the courts gave me. So i know that i got a year to do and if i want to work i can but i don't have to. Going through the process which i know and what to look for. I'm in building two. My first day on the yard I see the hoime Tear Rock he's in building three but he is working in the laundry room. we was able to talk for only a few minutes. me and four other homies are on the weight pile and the crips are on the other side getting their buff on. I don't know what it was but this big Homosexual asked me to be his man. I told him I don't get down like that. this is the biggest gay guy I ever seen. he got some twenty two inch arms and stood six feet five and two hundred and fifty pounds and a long pony tail in his hair. he got his clothes on very tight. I was told before hand on what he did to his cellie.

he said his name is CoCo and that his last cellie was sleeping and when he woke up CoCo had his dick in his mouth and CoCo said. " don't you move, i got this now get this hard for me." this was a crip dude that he done this to. no way i could have been in that cell with that big ass gay dude. I think i would have to take off on him if I woke up him holding my dick. I know he's big we would be in that cell fighting for our lives. And he asked me to be his man. no way this dude is taking dick. homies started laughing at me

BEHIND THESE WALLS

AND I'm laughing too.

Me and the homies had some words with the crips on our last two times out and we was about to beat them down and some how the c/o's found out. I was taken out my cell and escorted by two officers to the office. The sergeant said. " sit down Mr. Jones, i heard that you were out on the yard starting trouble with some other inmates. is that true?." " hell naw, i don't know what you're talking about." I said with anger in my voice. the Sergeant said. " well, there are more that four people saying that you was out there starting trouble. now Mr. Jones, i see how big you are and they feel threatened by you for whatever reason and i'm not about to have that on my yard. so i'm going to send you to the (SHU) Security Housing Unit. to keep you away from all the other guys. i see you only have one year to do, you might spend the rest of your time in the SHU. now it's up to your counselor you will be housed in "4-B" over there you can't scar all the other inmates. i don't know if you're doing or not i just can't keep you over here. so Mr. Jones, these two officers are going to escort you right right to the SHU. turn around so they can handcuff you. if you got anything in your cell, it will get to you. right now you got to go."
me and the two officers left the building. while i was in the office they let the homies outside for yard. I'm feeling like I'm back in the blood module the way I'm handcuffed. walking across the yard i see the homies working out on the weight pile. I said.

BEHIND THESE WALLS

" blood somebody dropped a hot kite on me saying that i made some threat's on the yard. i'm going to the SHU watch your back them dudes is lying to get people off the yard. I said my good bye's to them. I don't know if them crabs dropped that hot kite on me but we did get into it the other day. I do hope that the homies watch their backs them crabs might try and rat pack them now that I'm gone.

I get to the SHU. I never walked through so many door to get somewhere. i went through six doors, they made sure there is no way out of this hell hole the two c/o's walked me up stairs to a cell. I looked inside and i see this skinny black guy sitting on the bunk. I'm looking around and i only see ten to twelve cells and not many guys looking out their windows to see who just came in. the gun man opened the cell, i walked in and the door shut. one c/o opened up the food slot and i bent down and stuck out my hands to get the cuffs taken off. The c/o said. " Mr. Jones you will get your bed roll by dinner time." they walked away. I then walked over to the guy sitting on his smoking a cigarette I stuck out my hand and said. " I'm ru-al, what's up?." he said. " I'm Tony, hi." i notice that his voice sound kind of soft. I hope he's not gay. I had to ask. " say Tony are you gay?." he smiled and said. " yes I'm gay, i have been since 1970s, i live in Passadens and i have two brothers that are bloods. i can tell your a blood from your name, am I'm right?."

i said, " yeah, I'm a blood from Athens Park, but check this out I don't got anything against the gays, I just don't get down like that, so you give me respect and you will get yours. keep all the gay stuff to yourself and we won't have any problems. i just left this big ass guy dude on yard one, do you know him?." in his soft voice he said. " Oh! you met Co-Co, she's my girl, did you hear about the dick she took?." I said. " Yeah I heard about that, but can we stop talking about Co-Co and dicks?." I didn't want to talk about stuff like. Tony seen that i was getting upset and he changed the subject.

"Say, tony, tell me about the program in here i know that it can't be much of a program." I asked. Tony said. " We get let out of our cells for two hours a day, we get to watch T.V. and shower. It's only about fifteen guys in here. there is one other blood in here he's on the first tier. we all go to the chow hall together. we go to the store once a month we just went. we only get to spend $35.00 which is not much but it helps. No out side that is why we get the two hours of day room time. I'm here know four months I have eight years to do I should be gone from here in a week or two I'm going to do my time in Vacaville prison. I got some wooded Dominoes we can play when it get boring in here, but other than that welcome to the SHU.

It's dinner time and all the cell doors open. I followed Tony down the stairs and the first person i see is Frog. I have not seen him

PRISON LIFE

Since we was in Solano pen. I said " waht's up Blood?." I gave him a hug and he said. " ru-al, damn it's been long time , Blood you got big, what the fuck are you doing in here?." " blood, i think some crips dropped a hot kite on me. one day we was about to take off but it got squashed and the thing I know I'm being escorted over here. They said that I was a threat on the yard so here i am. so how did you get here? and how long you been here?" I asked. he smiled at me and said. " the same thing. someone dropped a hot kite on me and got me off the yard and i did get into it with some crabs on that yard before i came here. I've been in here for four months. i don't care, i only have a violation. Oh! you will be here for a while." I know been in here my points will go up to a level three or four and that's behind the walls.

I was able to kick it with Frog for three weeks before he left. I went to see my counselor and my points went up so when i leave the SHu i'm going to a level four. my points will go down in three months and I'll go to a level two if i don't fuck up in there.it won't matter what pen or level i go to I'll be welcome. today in the chow hall i seen this black guy we was told not to talk to them but have been anyway. I said " say bro is there and bloods where you're you housed? if so can you tell them that ru-al from A.P.B. send his love?." he said in a very low tone. " you got two home boys G-RAB and Pistol Pete, they are in the same cell in "4-A". I'll let them know that you send your love to them and that your over there." I said. " thank you bro.

PRISON LIFE

Four months has passed and three of then months I've been in this cell by myself and time is going by slow. if it wasn't for the letters from Judy and Cassandra it could have got stressful. this is a fucked up program. i hope to be gone soon if not, oh well i got to do it. I have seven months left and I don't want to do it here there is no weights push ups and jogging in place is keeping me fit and in shape.

I'm on the gray goose next stop Corcan prison. i heard about this prison when i was in Solano. it was one of many new prisons being built across this state and all the race riots that they was having but that's been three years ago I'm sure everything has calm down if not I'll be ready. it's just another pen and I'll be on top of my game.

I get there and it's built just like all the other new prisons. I'm in building "B" the orientation building. after three days i seen the counselor. he said. " Mr. Jones if you program for sixty days no write ups you can go to a level one yard. and it can be sooner than that, but for now you will be going to yard "C" today." I was cool with that at least i don't have to be in this building with nothing and i get to kick it with the homies.

Me and four other guys are walking on "C" yard to our building and i can feel the tension. I'm looking at the weight pile and this yard is made different from the other level three and four yards it's wide open no around the corner like Solano's. I don't see any home boys yet. I'm going to be on my toes, we get to building six

PRISON LIFE

And and I'm in cell twenty five. waiting on the gun man to open the cell door, only a few guys are i the day rood watching the big T.V. the door opens i walk in. I seen the light skinned guy through the door window he did look up at me while I'm waiting to get in. my first thought is he a crip. he better not disrespect me, if so i'm going to put him under the bunk until the next unlock. I said. " what's up bro? i'm ru-al from A.P.B.". not knowing if he bang or not i got to let him know where i'm from. he put out his hand and said. " west-up blood i'm Ears from Holly Hood Pirus."he got some yoke. i made up me bed and he got his T.V. on looking a Oprah. "say ru-al do you have a home girl Tanya that live in the dead end on Carlton street?." he asked. I said " yeah that's my home girl and my street. Say, Ears, what's up with the program?." no matter where I'm at behind these walls I got to know what's up with the program so i don't get caught up in the wrong thing and I know what I'm stepping out in. "it's a bool program we get our buff on, a lot of the homies got jobs. i don't have one yet. i got two years left to do. three weeks ago about five home boys from N.H.B. had rolled up their enemie. other than that it's been bool. there are some crabs from Bompton but they don't want any problems. we are on a black thang because the Mexicans they have been trying to flex their muscles so we are not tripping on banging on each other unless the crips get out of line. don't get me wrong blood we are not buddy buddy with them. if they got to get dealt with it's on. Dinner time will be in thirty minutes. and all the b-dogs walk there together

PRISON LIFE

After that we buff iron and just hang out."

After dinner we went to the weight pile. i met a lot of the homies and a few of them had heard about the drive-by that the crabs did on my family and killed my niece. they gave me some blood love and a few of them said that they put in some work for my loss when they heard it was a drive-by and a baby got killed. I felt all that love. I'm looking at this one b-dog hit eight quarters. i'm not that strong yet. I walked over to where he was and introduced myself to blood and he said. " i'm Little Dan from I.F.G." I said with a lot of excitement in my voice " you're Big Dan's little brother?. me and blood was cellies in Solano's together I bee you're strong like blood. but he was hitting ten quarters, put on seven for me let me see if i can hit it, i just came from the SHU with no weights."

I got under the seven quarters. Lil Dan is spotting me. i un-racked it and hit it three times and on the last one he had to help me get it back in the rack. it won't take me long to get my strength back. i know that I can hit it ten times for ten sets. blood got under it and hit it ten times with ease and he had them singing with every rep. he got up and smiled at me and i noticed that he's the strongest b-dog. after that me and Ears went to walk the track. I learned alot from blood about this yard and the homies. I see Reno but he didn't have that long jheri curl any more. we talked about our time in Solano's and walked the track until it was time to go in.

PRISON LIFE

Two months passed and i was moved to the level one yard it was a whole different world. this is so laid back. i see guys wearing slippers and laying on the grass. but i'm not going to let my guard down like that this is still prison.

I get to dorm "C" and the person i see is Dekume and then Socks and Lucky all them is from the Athens Park by way of the J-Block. we are four deep i never been this deep before and we are four deep from one hood. we hugged and they was happy to see me and we talked about the program on this yard and it was all good. "there are some crabs here but they don't any funk." Dekume said. this big ass young blood walked up and said. " I'm Lil Ness from V.N.G. and we got them crabs in check, but everybody is bool."

I end up getting a job in the kitchen working the breakfast shift I'm getting up at four thirty in the morning and all the homies are working getting their day for day. I'm bring all kinds of good food to the homies we are eating good everyday.

going in and out of the pen I'm meeting more girls and know i got this fine red bone Jamalah from the hood and she had found a way to call the door. at three o'clock on the dot the phone would ring and everyone knew it was for me. we would get our sex talk on all day and night that girl got a sexy ass phone voice.

Day one Dekume had been cooking spread. blood can cook. time went by so fast. Lil Ness, Socks and Lucky all had went home and i only have a month left. I have been buffing hard and know i got some

BEHIND THESE WALLS

Twenty one inch arms this is the biggest I ever been the more I come to prison the bigger I gets. Dekume cooked me my last big meal and it was good. it's time to say my good bye's. my sisters K-Dae and Connie is in the front to take me home and the got my two year old daughter Albanisha with them I'm going to spend some time with her i got to stop coming to prison and spend time with my daughter and Judy said that she is tired of me coming in and out of these prison but i just can't stay off them streets.

1992 I'm back in Chino, on the west yard and I'm glad that I'm not stuck in central in those cells. Me and G-Rab got caught up in a robbery and got receiving stolen property and took a deal and once again my violation will eat up the sixteen months. I'm in Fern dorm this time with eight other bloods. I met them all and this tall blood said." I'm Tree from Tree Top Pirus (TTP) you got a home boy Zell in Elm dorm, when you're done making up your bed and putting up your things I'll take you to him.

I walked outside and Zell was already here to greet me. we gave up some big hugs it felt good to see someone from the same street and grew up together. he is here for a ninety day opt from the courts on a murder case that he should beat. Blood is one of the rich ballers from our hood. and i know that Gangsta Mike got blood him a paid lawyer.

It's hot and sunny and just me and Zell is walking the track. we walked past this guy. Zell said. "ru-al we just passed up Humphery

BEHIND THESE WALLS

Your brother." I said "no we didn't, blood. I know my own brother even though I have not seen him in years." If i was on the streets he was in prison and if he was out I was in prison. We turned around to walk back. we got behind him and I said " say Humphery." The person turned around and true enough it is him, we looked at each other and smile and we started to hug each other very tight. this is our first time in the same prison together. he don't gang bang so he kick it where-ever he want to. He still got his nineteen inch arms. I had caught up with him in size and passed him up. but he is still my big brother. He gave Zell a hug and said " Dama, man, we walked right by each other and didn't even know it." I said " Zell seen you and didn't believe him when he said that was you." humphery has been doing time since 1978 in Y.A. and he haven't stopped coming to prison. We walked the track a few times and we're talking about old times, he had to go because he works in the kitchen. I said. " bring me some food. I'm in Fern dorm, okay?." He smiled and said " alright, I'll be there after chow."

I'm chillen in the day room, I've been here three weeks now. This time is going good. no problem with the Crips. I looked at the door and there's Zell. i can see something was wrong. He said " ru-al check this, blood, these crabs in my dorm are acting Brazy and talking shit . Since I'm the only B-dog in there they think I'm some kind of punk so get the other homies and roll with me. I'm going to call out this crab with his big mouth. I don't want

PRISON LIFE

Them crabs to try and rat pack me." Zell didn't lift any weights he stood five foot eight and real dark skinned. I know that he can fight. I know that he would have been shot that crab if he was on the streets. we did go on one mission together and we put in some work on them crabs. So a squabble he got no problem with that.

We get to the dorm and it's about five of us. and i see six to seven crabs standing at the front door of his dorm. My heart is beating fast. it's about to be on with these crabs. the homie Tree said " I hear that Y'all have a problem whit our home boy Zell. if so, you know there's a place that they can get down head up, because there is not going to be any rat packing. so what's up?." this short crab spoke. " we don't have any problem with Zell. it was a big misunderstanding on my home boy's part and we talked to him and he wants to apologize to him there is no problem any more." The dude said his apology and Zell accepted it and we went our way. the homie Tree handled that perfectly. i know that I would have wanted to ride on them crabs. I don't have no respect for them crabs after they did that drive - by and murder my niece LIL China so I'm not giving any passes and the homies will have to ride or just kick back because they made it real personal when them cowards did that. But I did like the way the homie Tree handled that. a few new home boys drove up and they are C/K riders. sitting in the day room watching T.V. it's a good movie on. everyone is into it. no one is talking while the movie is on.

PRISON LIFE

After the movie was over this guy turned to a talk show and it was showing this man hitting this two year old girl with his fist. it was a disgusting sight to see. then they showed it over and over. this dude is sitting between me and the homie LIL Snaps from the Pueblos and right behind us is Monster Herb from P9. that dude started laughing at the child being hit by that grown man. We seen that he was laughing at the child getting hit. and the next time I knew the homie Snaps knocked him out right where he was standing. He did it so fast neither me or Monster Herb had a chance to to react to him. now he is laying on the floor and I'm looking around to see if he has any home boys that might want to help him but no-one stepped up for him. Snaps said " laugh now you bitch, you can't because your knock the fuck out. i bet you won't laugh ay another child being hit by a buster." He got up and walked to the bathroom to fix up his face. he then went to the C/O office and told them that he couldn't live in this dorm any more. he packed up his things and left. he didn't snitch.

Humphery caught the chain and Zell went back to the county jail to fight his murder case. I'm glad that I was able to spend some time with them. I hope to see them when I get out.

I'm on the Gray Goose bus on my way to Chuckawalla prison the ride was nice I have seen just about the whole state riding on these prison buses we do have a nice looking state. after the five-hour drive we pulled up to the prison that inmates call "Chucky's House". we go through the big gates. this prison is in the middle

PRISON LIFE

OF THE DESERT. I got off the bus and the heat hit me right in the face it's hot as hell it got to be well over a hundred degrees and it's January. I'm going to a level one yard. we went to R&R and then to building "C". I seen a lot of guys on the weight pile. I didn't see anyone i know. I got my bed made up and this guy walked up to me and said. " what's up I'm Gramps from C.M.G. where are you from Blood?." I looked at him he stood about six foot three and he got some size on him. I said. " I'm ru-al from A.P.B. so what's up with the program?." He said. " It's bool there are some crabs here we got them in check and any one of them want to get down we have a good blind spot where we won't get caught. other than that we are programing. Oh I know that your wondering how I knew you was a B-dog, well you got that Damu look and walk blood."

I get outside and I greet all the homies and I notice that a lot of the bloods are from San Diego. Konrad from Sky Line Piru's, Elm, Wiggles and Drackrula all from Lincon Park Bloods and it's about five more little home boys from their hoods and they are called "Termites" like we in Los Angeles call our young homies Y.G.B.'s I had heard that this pen and Donovan prison is like their headquarters. I know that they have some down b-dogs out of San Diego.

Me and Wiggles has become real close it was that Park love. since I don't have to work I can kick back but I want to get a job. I did and i became a door porter cleaning up the dorm I got morning shift. The job is keeping me moving. Wiggles is going to school

PRISON LIFE

to get his time cut in half. He is one of the tallest homies with some nineteen inch arms. we would stay up late night and talk about our "crack" smoking days. I'm getting two care packages and we are cooking just about everyday. I got my twenty-one inch arms and I'm hitting eight quarters. I do have my ego in check I'm not out to be the biggest on the yard like I used to do.
here three months and no drama and that's good. i like it here. today I got to call Judy. now i only call home once a month that's to keep the bills down. But I want to see if she sent my care package no matter what Judy made sure that I eat good in here. I have been in and out of prisons and she has been down with me through it all. I know this is getting old for her and I got to get my life together because if I don't I'm going to lose a good woman. I know that she is getting tired of this. I got to make a change when I get out this time. I got a girl that really loves my black ass.
RING! RING! " Collect call form AL, Hold please." the operator said. damn that operator sound sexy. " I have a collect call from AL will you accept?." she said. "yes" Judy said. I said " hey baby how are you doing today?." She spoke in her soft sweet voice "I'm doing fine Albert." I know when she call me by my whole name something is wrong. Judy said " before you say anything I have some sad news to tell you, your daddy passed away two days ago your mamma called me and told me to tell you when you call me.

PRISON LIFE

Your mamma said " he died from Lung Cancer and Diabetes in the hospital."Albert I'm sorry for your lost I know how close you and your daddy were." "wow daddy is dead." I said with tears rolling down my face, all kinds of memories with him started going through my mind and all of them are good ones. it seem like three minutes has passed before i said anything and Judy let me do my thinking and I know she can hear me crying. she broke the silent and said. Albert it's going to be okay, baby you want me to call your mamma on the three way for you?." I said " yes please."

"hi, Mamma, how are you doing today?." I said with a choked up voice. Mamma said. " son I'm doing okay. it's hard to believe that Jones has passed away. Oh i tell you, your daddy put up a fight. he gave them doctors and nurses hell, he had took the I.V. needle out his arms about five time wanting to walk out of there. He is in a good place now, Albert your daddy did his wrong in this world but he was a God fearing man and he loved his family and took care of us. We should have checked on his high sugar level because then we could have done something about it and we missed out and knowing that his brother your uncle Leon passes from the same thing. so know everybody is getting checked and you get checked while your in there too. it happen close to his 67th birthday. So it's a sad time for the Jones family. the good kids are going to do all the funeral arrangements. so we'll be there. so how are you doing in your second home?." I said " I'm doing fine Mamma, I know that I got to get my life together because Judy deserve better than what I'm doing. she has been so good to me. I got to make a change in my life for her and our kids. I'm going to get off this parole this time."

Mamma said " you do have a good women in Judy and if you don't get yourself together they are going to lock you up forever. so it's up to you son. The whole family sends their love to you and will tell your daddy that you love him. now boy let me get off this phone and you be good in there. I love you Albert." I said " i love you too Mamma." Before she hung up she gave Judy a thank you and some love, and Judy sent that same love back. Judy said " AL, what did you Mamma mean what she said "the good kids?." I said " that's what she call my half brothers and sisters. Well, let me get off the phone Judy. I'm very serious about this change because i love you so much. I do know how good I got it with you, and i know i can do better with my life. I'll be home in three months. so have my T-bone steak dinner ready for me and you know what I want for my dessert." Judy got the last words. she said " I love you so much and I'm sorry for the loss of your daddy. Please don't get into any trouble, i know you stupid face i want you home on your release day." I said " okay I love you you give my love and hello to my mother-in-law and the rest of the family. by by".

I'm walking around the track by myself I didn't tell none of the homies about my lost yet. not to many guys outside a few are walking the track. I'm clearing my head as I reminisce on some of the good and fun times I had with daddy. I hate that I'm not home to be with my family. tears are flowing down my face. my daddy rest in peace. I cleared my face i don't want anyone to see me crying. the tears had dried up anyway because of this hot ass weather. I see why not too many guys are out side but i need to be outside right now. I need to smoke a joint. I'll get at the homie Elm later he'll look out for me. I'm getting my walk on and i thought of something that me and Pops done and I'm smiling. as I'm walking these two crips walked by me and one of them had this mean look on his face and he was looking right at me. my happy thoughts went out my mind and my thoughts went to anger, and i felt that crab disrespected me.

I stopped and then they stopped and I said " what the fuck are you looking at?." The bigger crip spoke " because i want to cuzz, what are you going to do about it?." This crab just don't know how much anger i got built up inside me right now. I could tear some shit up right now. Judy just said don't anything stupid. well that's out the window I'm about to fuck this crab up. I seen him on the weight pile i don't know his name, hell I don't know any of them crabs names. I said with a half smile and half smerk on my face. "let's go to a neutral dorm and i'll beat your crab ass." he said "let's go you slob."

We walked to the neutral dorm and i didn't tell none of the homies

BEHIND THESE WALLS

that I'm about to fight this crab. and if they try to rat pack me I know that I can handle two at one time. this dorm has a good blind spot his home boy sat at the far table to keep watch. I took off my jacket and T-shirt. he took off his as well. he got some size on him too. I'm thinking oh hell, yeah, that's cool I might can get a good fight. he was about to say something but before he could get the words out I socked him in the nose and it started bleeding. his head went back and i came in with another punch I tried to knock him out but I missed. he got his balance back and we squared up. blood is pouring out of his nose, I wasn't happy with i want to put him in some pain. i stuck a left jab out there to see if i could get him to make the wrong head move so I can knock him out but he didn't bite on the bait. so I punched him in the stomach and he felt that. he got in a good punch on the top of my head but it didn't faze me but the second punch caught me on the jaw. i backed up to get my vision back and he let me. I thought for sure he would be all on me and that's where he fucked up at. I came with a left and then a right hook and i caught him right on the chin and it was lights out. he hit the floor with a solid thump. his head hit the floor and i stood over him i see the blood coming from his nose and a big ass knot growing on his forehead. i grabbed my shirt and jacket, as i was walking out the cube his home boy walked in and he looked down and then at me. he had this fear look in his eyes and i looked at him with no words "YOU DON'T WANT NONE".

BEHIND THESE WALLS

I'm walking to my dorm and sweat is dripping of my body like someone poured water on me. I said to my self " now that was a good fight i got hit a few times and got the knockout . I'm bool now. i took off my stocking cap i had to cover up my long pony tails so he don't try to grab one of them and do me bad.

Once in my dorm I walked over to Wiggles bunk. he is laid back looking at T.V. he is in the same spot when i was on the phone. he said " blood why is you so sweaty like that? you was getting your buff on without me?." I said " Naw, gangsta, i wasn't getting my buff on. I just beat down a crab in that neutral dorm, that's why I'm sweating like this." he got off his bunk and said " why didn't you come get me ru-al?. you know you got to come get your boy. what crab was it?." I said " it was the one that had that walk and some yokes. Blood i didn't have time to come get you. you seen me on the phone earlier i was talking to Judy and my Mamma and they had told me that my Pops had passed. so i went outside to get some fresh air and while I was walking i passed two crabs and one of them was red eyeing me and you know how i am about that. so i called him out and we went into the dorm and i knocked him out. he got me with a couple good ones but he got fucked up. your going to hear about it later on. it was head up and it felt good too." I'm looking at wiggles and know he want to fight someone he's all pumped up. "damn, ru-al, i just seen you all that happen that fast?. let's go outside." he said. I said " hold up blood let me shower first just in case that dude told on me at least i won't look like I've been in a fight."

BEHIND THESE WALLS

Me and wiggles went outside and I see some crips had grouped up and there are some homies over there talking to them. we get over there and Gramps is talking to one of them. I'm just listening to Gramps talk. I spoke up. " blood it was head up, he got knock out if he want so get back we can do it again i have no problem with that fade. Gramps you don't need to explain shit to them, dude was in the wrong and he got dealt with and he had his home boy right there. he kept watch." the crip dude said "naw, ru-alit's all squash we are not trying to kick anything off with Y'all. my home boy lost the fight head up and it's over. we respect that big bro."

We went to our hang out spot on the yard and Gramps said " ru-al you know your brazy, you bee that crab face, blood you fucked him up." Everybody started laughing. I told the homies that I lost my Pops. right then Elm pulled out five fat ass joints and we got high and enjoyed the rest of the day.

Three new homies drove up T.S. from Lincon Park, Bucky from my hood and China Man from C.M.G. and to see him after our time together in C.M.C. prison. it felt good to have some new b-dogs, it seem like when a few leave we get some more. China Man and the young homie from Lincon Park is putting a big tattoo on blood back he's getting "Inglewood" and it looked like it hurt. I cooked up a big spread and China Man wanted to do the next one and I know that he got cooking skills. With these big spreads it's bring us closer.

BEHIND THESE WALLS

China Man have been shooting dice and winning I know on the streets and every hood picnic or hood party I've been to I seen blood gambling so this is his thing. he got his locker and two other homies locker full of canned good and cartons of cigarettes and he got photo ducats and funny money so when we need to go to night store we used that funny money. He got this group of five guys that he gamble with everyday after dinner. they got their pillow cases of all kind or can goods each one is a dollar and other kinds of good cookies, bags of chips and crackers anything that can be eaten and worth more that a dollar it's money. China Man said " ru-al this is like in the hood. I'm bucking these fools." I laugh he got that look like everything is going well on the streets there it's thousands of dollars on the ground and everyone has a pistol that's why i don't gamble like they do., but here it's more control but it still can get ugly. the table has turned this night China Man is losing he took all the food and packs of smokes out of everyone lockers and he's down to his ten can goods. he put them all up and the guy hit his point. me and Wiggles is watching this crip dude win all our stuff and we don't like that at all. The crip dude went to his locker to put up the pillow cases of food into his locker.

I said " come on Wiggles, let's go get our stuff back." We walked over to dude's locker and he was standing there trying to find room in his locker to stuff our shit. Wiggles said. " say bro, give my homie action to win his money back. you just can't lock up on his stuff and not give him so get back. So what your going to do?." We are standing by his locker he got hundreds of canned good and about seven cartons of cigarettes. there is no way I'm going to let him keep all our stuff. I said "so what are you going to do, are you going to give him some get back?." He filled a pillow case of canned good and smokes and if he lose all that or China Man don't have no more it's over. he said " tell China Man to bring the dices." We walked off to tell blood what we did and china Man was ready I gave him all my canned goods and a few other homies did too. Wiggles said " that dude bet not win because it's going to get very ugly real fast."

China man and dude are in the cube and they are going at it. we got the lookout for the guards because if they get caught they are going to the hole. the homie is bucking him he got stack of can goods. he got sweat coming down his face. He know have two pillow cases filled up the crip dude went to his locker twice the homie is putting work in getting our stuff back and it's close to yard re-call and then it's over with. the crip dude lost everything he had. He said " China Man I'm done with this gambling shit." He walked away and we didn't care if he was mad we just wanted our stuff back the next day we cooked a big spread.

My last day behind these walls and I hope forever. we got high on some bomb ass weed. I never did drink pruno but the homies got drunk they made some that do taste just GIN. everybody is feeling good on my last night we got the food cooked and the music bumping loud we are having a hood party we are taking photos of this time together. the homies is telling me how I need to marry Judy because they know how good of a women she is and I told them that I would when I get off parole. we ate a good meal and it's fifteen homeboys and they are sending me out proper.

Time for me to go home I know that my Judy got the red candles and big meal waiting on me to walk through the door and I'm going to make love to my girl all night long. I'm being escorted to the gate and I said " okay gangsta Y'all b-up, and I'll bee you on the streets. and don't trip I'm going to hook up them two care packages and it's going to be good. Wiggles know what to do when they get here. " Looked at them and gave them my last hug and Wiggles said " PARK LOVE RU-AL". I hope that 1993 is the last of the prison life BEHIND THESE WALLS.

BEHIND THESE WALLS

THE COURT SYSTEM

being poor is a bad thing, but being poor and black is even worse in these courts we are given a lawyer that is supposed to help you get your freedom back from a crime you did or didn't do. if you don't have the money to hire your own lawyer the state will provide one for you. this is your rights as a citizen of the Unite States Of America. these lawyers went to school to learn the law on how to beat cases. and they are suppose to work for you. but it don't happen that way. the states appointed lawyers are also trained to make sure that you don't get out but make it look like they are putting up a big fight for you. and there's the paper work to show that they put up a good defense for you with their big lawyer words. we're sitting in that seat not knowing what the hell they are talking about. and they is not going tell us because it's not school time, so the words fly right over our heads. when it's all said and done, we either take a deal or we are found guilty in a trial. and then your off to prison on a case that you know that you could have won if you had a paid lawyer.

The court's job is to make sure it's a fair fight between the lawyers and the District Attorney's and nine out of ten times you and your lawyers lose. How can that be when they went to the same kind of schools. is the D.A. smarter than your lawyer?. or have they made a deal behind closed doors and go play golf together after you're gone off to prison and not even think about what they just done with your life?. if the tax payers is giving the state money out of their checks to represent to poor shouldn't them lawyer's put up a better fight to keep you out of prison?. since most people come out the ghetto or low class neighborhoods they think we won't be missed by our loved ones. is that ghetto justice, JUST-US?.

If your in that hot seat and your dump truck lawyer it's best you start making your plans for prison and try to get the best deal you can with less time. if you depending on a jury to set you free good, luck. because no matter what kind of case you got it could could be murder or just a petty theft case they are going to look at you as guilty because most free people think you're in that hot seat for a reason you done it. them thought's comes to their minds even before the trial beings. so you're in a no win situation. you may have big action if you have a paid lawyer because he or she is on your team and not like a state appointed lawyer friendly with the D.A. I have this to say about our court system.

                    I'M GUILTY UNTIL I
                CAN PROVE MY INNOCENCE!!!

BEHIND THESE WALLS

HOMEBOYS & HOMEGIRLS
BROTHERHOOD & SISTERHOOD

A homie is someone you grew up with from the same neighborhood. they are the ones you and trust with your life because you know them and grew up with them and that's where that bond is built and that love. all hoods have this special bond with their gang family. bloods on the streets can go into that hood and be welcome with a lot of love no matter what that need may be that blood love is there. but we need to go a bit farther than just that love on the streets. there are many homeboys and homegirls in these prisons that still need that love so I say this blood. If you have a homei in one of these prisons stop for a moment and show some love it only takes about fifteen minutes to write a letter and let them know that they are loved and not forgotten and to keep their heads up. A letter from a homie from the streets can go a long ways to ones mental behind these walls. So I say this find one homie get his hook and surprise them with some positive words because most feel that they are being forgotten and not loved any more. As i got out of prison many of times i didn't get one letter but when i got home that's when I got the love. So don't let the word HOME mean just that you got to home to get that homie love. Don't leave your RAD'S for dead in these hell holes.

BEHIND THESE WALLS

When I first walked behind these walls I was showed a lot of brotherhood love and that really surprised me because they was not from my gang. The love I got from all these different bloods from blood hoods I never heard of but was as one brotherhood and the respect that was given out. I loved being a blood even more. and when those O.G.'s put me under their wings and taught and showed me how to conduct myself as a blood behind these walls I had to pass it on to those that would listen. But i know that them O.G.'s didn't have to do that but they seen that I would be able to pass on that same love because it's so hard to be a blood being out number five to one by crips we need each other in every way on the streets and behind these walls.

PRISON LIFE

DAMUISM

A BROTHERHOOD AND SISTERHOOD OF
WARRIORS CONNECTED BY VALUES AND
BELIEF, AND ASSOCIATION OF
INTELLIGENT VIRTUOUS MEN AND
WOMEN UNDER THE ORDER OF
SOLDIERY, AN INDESTRUCTIBLE STRUCTURE.
BLOOD LOVE.

PRISON LIFE

"CALIFORNIA PRISONS"

This is a state that has more prisons than universities, and we're just a few prisons away from outnumbering the community colleges as well. this state is wrapped around by prisons like barbed wire. the city streets are the yards. there is this saying about this state. " if you come to California for vacation you will leave or stay on probation."

Mamma was right, this has become my second home. I have been doing this time as if I was happy to do but I was not. like so many others this has become our second home. the state is building these prisons like a human wear house to hold us. there are close to two hundred thousand men and women in these human wear house's and more to come. I was told by an L.A. county Sheriff said " this is a revolving door it always will open and close for you" I never thought about them words until my third time in prison this is a revolving door. The two things that we as gang members are doing is filling up prisons and graveyards.

PRISON LIFE

PRISON ROLL CALL

C.C.I., C.I.M., C.I.W., C.M.C., C.R.C., C.C.W., C.C.F., AVENAL, CORCORAN, CALIPATRIA, CENTINELA, CHUCKAWALLA, CHINO, COALINGA, DELANO, DONOVAN, FOLSOM, HIGH DESERT, IRONWOOD, JAMESTOWN, KERN VALLEY, LANCASTER, MULE CREEK, PLEASANT VALLEY, PELICAN BAY, SALINAS VALLEY, SIERRA, SOLANO, SOLEDAD, STOCKTON, SUSANVILLE, SAN QUENTIN, TAFF, TEHACHAPI, TRACY, VACAVILLE, WASCO, AND ALL FEDS.

For all the homeboys and homegirls that's behind these walls, stay strong and don't let them get you down because these prison are designed to mess with your mental state and drive you crazy. if the state can get you on their medication, you're really going to lose your mind. so you see how much you need your homie's to stay sane. always remember where you came from. don't trip on how you got here but find a way out because it can done. I be damned if ru-al just give up. I know it's easy to get in and hard to get out. That's why I always keep this in my head " I do time, I don't let time do me."

Homies, while we're in these prisons don't just sit in them cells find something to do with your time. get into some kind of school. since most of us didn't go to school on the streets we can get our education in here. now we have all the time in the world to study and do that homework. with working with your mind and not just thinking about this hell hole it will help you stay out the hole and trouble and in other people business. I know that you can get your G.E.D. and some prisons you can get a college degree too. Or you can get into a religious course and that what I love to do study other religions and why do people choose the faith that they believe in. I'm working on a religion theology degree and i know I want to understand it and my faith is strong and Jesus. with no shame. I will always have love for the Blood car. So homies find that solace with in yourself and keep an open mind and love your RADS. but it all comes to you on how you want to do your time. you can make it easy or hard on your self. it's your choice. you're stuck right know. I'm going to make the best of my time because I know that I'm going to be walking out of this place. I hope that you have that same attitude. these prisons are going to be here a long time after we're gone but what we leave behind is our legacy and I want mines to be tight. I know I have made many mistakes and without them I couldn't have learn. when I leave this earth i want to be known as a down blood, not a hard one but a down one.

I know we all lost some good homies behind these walls and they wasn't able to walk out. I send my best regards to you and your blood family. Just as on the streets we are going to lose some homies in here and that's sad that some got to die in here. let's not forget them and what they put into this B-car. we got to die someday and if it's in here make sure you have made peace with your maker because i am and have. I said it once and I'll say it again don't give up on your faith no matter what your religion faith may be it can humble you in hard times and yes gangsta do go to heaven.

I know it hurts to lose love ones while your in prison and not able to see your kids grow up and your grandkids. we are missing out on so much and it eats at you in a way that you blame yourself but don't yes you me made our life choices but somethings we can't change and we must find the best way to deal with it. and to have your homies to talk to and get that comfort you need at sad times. don't give up bloods behind these walls.

PRISON LIFE

"NOW ON S.O. DEATH ROW"

Sitting here on death row for a crime I did do. but these are the cards that was dealt to me. This is supposed to be my last stand, I'm at the bottom of the prison chain. You can't get no lower that death row i have been to every prison level that is in this corrupt prison system and here i am on the row. they want to ex ru-al out the game in a real way. But i do practice what I preach. I'm going to give them the sad face or why me I know what i got to do to keep ru-al on point. Yeah I got to wake up every morning knowing that the state want to kill me and my homies. but I wake up every morning and say my prayers and it's on me to be positive and productive.

to see some guys that i have been with for many of years get executed and it's a crazy thing to witness it can really touch your soul. that is what they want to do to me. in and out of these prison most of my adult life i never thought that i would end up on death row. I'm not going to give up. It do brings alot of a perspective on one's life and what he have done on this earth. I some homies up here that we have a very strong bond and it's real love. with out each other it would be hard on some of us, but we are as one in a real way. I even done some growing up myself. I didn't come up here to gang bang I got my street rep and my prison rep so i have nothing to prove on how down I am. I know how to do the brotha thing as well, this is the closest I've ever been around crips and i knew that i had to adjust because each and everyone of us is here to get executed. I knew that i had to adjust to this place and the way it's set up. If a gang member didn't get their rep in another prison or on the streets this is the wrong place for it. yes if someone cross that line I'll defend myself and I'm very good at that but I'm not out looking for it like was in my younger days, this life on the row is a whole different level of living. the crips do their thang and we do ours. but it's still gangsta blood with me. I know it's more of a respect thing in here and there are a few crips that I do talk too and they are some good brotha's but i know who they are and my guard will not be let down. There are a chosen few that i like talking to but if i need to talk so bad i have my homies for that and my Northern brothas.

Being in this one man cell i got time to reflect on my life and what I'm going to do with it. I know that I got action to get out this bottom less pit. and I'm staying busy while I'm here. no matter how bad it may seem is got my home boys and we got each other.

Know it's time for our street homeboys and homegirls to step up and show that blood love. I'm sure that you know that you have a homie on the row these people want to kill you boy, is that bool with you?. Blood pick up a pen and paper and get at us. this is when we need that blood love from you. don't wait until they murder your homie and then go to the funeral and cry and say how much love me or other homies in these prisons. we need some smiles and laughter now. As for me being on the row the last two years I have been getting that love from G-Man and his wife Yolanda, Baby Girl "Tanya" and the homie her husband Melvin "Mel Dog" the homie Paul "P-Rock" Gary "Socks" Moore these are the homies that came into my life and has helped me deal with this. It took 23 years but it was right on time and I love them for that. I get to call them whenever I want to. I know other homies that have love ones in these prison can show that same love. We don't want much but conversation and to reminisce of our time together on the streets. So I say thank you for that homies love.

I started write about my gangsta life back in 2000 and it's know 2019 this part I'm adding so you can understand what i have been doing in my one man cell. I have five books of my life two of them are already on Amazon which I self published I have my death row cook book "our last meals" and one of my two death row autobiography "I'm In God's Confinement" that is a big accomplishment for me. this gangsta book on my life in prison and my street gangsta book "10 Toez Down" and my second death row book "Put On The Shelf To Die" which all three of them books go together and these books are my life and my legacy and every name in these books is apart on my legacy. So being in this one man cell i have written five book and I also have an eight book series of Christian children books. So for 20 years of writing I have found my niche in a place that want to suck your soul out of your body. So this why I say don't give up because you still be a factor in this world even if your on death row or a level one yard make your legacy yours and worth talking about 100 years from now.

I do say this, it's blood on mines until I'm six feet under or cremated and if it happen in here i know i did it my way. So the Damu's on the row do send our love to the homies in the pen we are family and to all the homeboys and homegirls in b-dog hoods your needed in these pens as well as our allies. B-UP.

BEHIND THESE WALLS

S.O. DAMU ROLL CALL

RU-AL A.P.B., DRU F.T.P., G-WAYNE F.T.P., YOUNG FAT RAT L.H.P., J-ROCK I.F.G., JUVENILE C.M.G., PEE-WEE F.S.G., BIG FAT RAT F.S.G., BIG TIME F.S.G., ASE KAPONE V.N.G., DANNY BOY V.N.G., SPREG B.H., BABY GANGSTA B.H., MARIO B.H. DEE-DOGG B.H., TAKO B.H., D-WAYNE B.P.S., K.I. L.P.B., M.P. S.L.P., S.B. S.L.P., P-FUNK L.P.P., MONSTER HERB P9, Y.B. P9, SUNDAY SHOES P9, CRICKET 30 PIRU, ROCK 30 PIRU, KAT WALK L.P.P., MOE F.T.B.,.

To our allies the Bay Area brothas and our brown skin S.A. brothas we have built a bond in all these pens that has lasted for many of years. That love and trust that we have for each other do make us shine even in the darkest places. And if I forgot your name in any of the roll calls you know that you was there so you can speak on it. so I say keep the fight and know that your loved some where and your not alone because we are one BEHIND THESE WALLS.

BEHIND THESE WALLS

MY PRISON PRAYER

Dear Lord, thank you for protecting me as i walked through these prison doors. when things got rough you was there to help me and guide me. I know that you has blessed me with that special angel to look over me in here, as you did for me on the streets. I knew when I got baptized in Chino prison there was no shame I wanted and needed your protection in your loving grace. and i notice that you kept me alive and unharmed behind these dark walls for a reason. I'll never denied your love for me and that your my Lord and savior. I do give all my props to you Lord first. Lord, I pray that you keep looking over my homeboys and homegirls that's locked up because we do need your mercy. if being on death row is my last stop on this earth I ask for a long life and a good peace of mind and healthy. I also ask that you Lord continue to forgive me of my sins because I'll never be perfect but your love and protection I ask in your Holy name BEHIND THESE WALLS, AMEN. John 14:6

EPILOGUE

the first time i heard that steel door slam shut behind me was in Carson sub station. I wasn't scared or nervous. I was more afraid of what Mamma and daddy was going to do to me. When Mamma said "Albert if you don't get your life together these people are going to lock you up forever and not think twice about it.

Not taking Mamma's advice, I found myself in L.A. county jail that's when i felt for the first time that uneasy feeling in my stomach. I heard about this place and how guys would get rape and beat up. when I walked through these doors I knew that I was in for an experience of a lifetime. as i entered behind these walls over and over again somehow I got immune to seeing and hearing guys get their manhood taken away and beat down for some reason I kept coming back and each time i learned to live in such harsh conditions.

To take orders from another man or women and being told when you can eat, sleep, shower, shit, piss and when to speak. I lost all them freedoms. I have no more control of my life anymore. How did I get immune to something like this?. it's so barbaric. I asked myself many times why didn't i listen to my parents. someone that loves me and cares for me. but i allowed myself to be told what to do by people that don't even know me. and it i decide not to listen to them i could get a beat down or punished put in the hole. have i let these pigs and guards become my parents?.

once i accepted this life style i had to make some very serious adjustments. first I had to learn to avoid the harsh part of this discomfort, with the grooming from the O.G.'s on how to deal with this lifestyle. and how to make your time behind these walls as easy as possible. I was all ears when they spoke. i know if I'm going to make this a part of my life i got to make sure that ru-al be able to walk out these doors smarter, alive and with my dignity and a man and a down b-dog.

I never forgot the words that my big homie big Mouse said. " ru-al, you do the time and don't let the time do you". at first I didn't know what he meant by that. when I did realized what it meant I knew it's up to me on how i want to to do my time.

I lost most of my fights in the Blood module and that was a learning process for me and what to come doing my time in these prisons. I never lost a fight with a crip or any other blood I see that I had to take my lumps to get better. but fighting crips it was something that bought out the anger in me. I could have met my match but I never did so i never underestimate anyone big or small. but when it came to fighting them crips it brought out the best in me and i had to take off first to make sure I win.

once i got to prisons i had to control that anger because in here the stakes are much higher. you can really get killed and brought to your knees. I had to take everything I learned in the module and take it up to a bigger level. one thing about me I didn't start shit but I know how to end it. I respect others and I knew I

BEHIND THESE WALLS

knew that i had to in order to get it back. When I had my encounters with them crips i felt disrespected so i dealt with them. and I wanted head up I didn't need no other homie to jump in that's the crips thing "RAT PACK" only help me if I hit the ground.

I give my utmost respect to all b-gods and our allies. anyone outside the car they got what they had coming form me. I always made my own enemies which are crips, and if i had to fight another blood we get down and that is it with no love lost no matter the outcome. I never made myself an enemy to another blood and I'm going to keep it like that.

one thing I never done behind these walls and that's smoke "CRACK" rocks. I know how crazy i get on the streets and in here when onew is on drugs he lose some respect and do them streets things and it's hard to get away when you flip your wig on getting high. Know I love my weed and that I laugh and eat junk food and enjoy myself. and when it's time to really get down and your high you can't function and you could get yourself and other hurt. And when it breaks out one would wonder where was you when the smoke cleared?.

This lifestyle is not for everyone. you can become the prey the day you walk through that door or walk on that yard because there are some hard core predators waiting on you and most of them are booty bandits and they will take your manhood and make you their bitch.

BEHIND THESE WALLS

Mamma always said that prison was my second home and it became just that. But think that she was happy that I was in prison at times because many of the himies was getting killed on the streets. But she knew that I could handle myself in here but on the streets anything goes. and she know being in here I'm still alive. and she is able to get a good night sleep and knowing I won't be getting shot up or killed which i had almost a few times but is knew me being in prison she felt I was safe.

I made my own choices in these prisons and i never got under any paper work as my big homie suggested i not do. I got out and got out but i kept coming back. I have a good women in Judy that put up with all my craziness but she hung in there with her stupid face. I knew one day that would try to weld my door shut and they have I'm on death row but I see some cracks in the weld. I don't blame no-one for my life style. And I don't knock the ones that hung their red flags up because they did it their way and respected and honor it. When I'm ready to hang mines up I'm going to do it on my terms but for know I see a lot of positive things I can do with the young people on this gang life and why it's not worth getting in because you will miss out on a life on the other side of this moment of fun. so for know I'm going to keep it gangsta BEHIND THESE WALLS!!!.

Printed in Great Britain
by Amazon